'MY DEAR ONE', A VICTORIAN COURTSHIP

'MY DEAR ONE'

A Victorian Courtship

THE LETTERS OF AGNES BOWERS
AND ARTHUR THORNDIKE

———

WITH THE BEGINNINGS OF AN
AUTOBIOGRAPHY
BY SYBIL THORNDIKE CASSON

———

EDITED BY PATRICIA CASSON
POSTSCRIPT BY JOHN CASSON

Julia MacRae

A DIVISION OF FRANKLIN WATTS

First published in Great Britain 1984 by
Julia MacRae Books, a division of Franklin Watts
12a Golden Square, London W1R 4BA
and Franklin Watts Inc
387 Park Avenue South, NY10016
and Franklin Watts Australia
1 Campbell Street, Artarmon, N.S.W. 2064

Designed by Douglas Martin

British Library Cataloguing in Publication Data

My dear one.
1. Thorndike, Arthur   2. Actors – Great
Britain – Biography
I. Casson, Patricia
792'.028'0924   PN2598.T55   m9   1984

ISBN 0–86203–185–0 UK edition
ISBN 0–531–09773–0 US edition
Library of Congress Catalog Card No: 84-61214

Printed and bound in Great Britain
by the Pitman Press Limited, Bath

CONTENTS

ACKNOWLEDGEMENTS, VI

ILLUSTRATIONS, VII

INTRODUCTION, II

———

THE BEGINNINGS OF AN AUTOBIOGRAPHY
BY SYBIL THORNDIKE CASSON, 17

———

THE LETTERS OF AGNES BOWERS
AND ARTHUR THORNDIKE, 27

———

POSTSCRIPT, 157

ACKNOWLEDGEMENTS

In putting together these letters I would like to express my gratitude to Judy Hough for her enormous enthusiasm, help, and advice, and to my husband, John Casson, my son-in-law, Tom Pocock, and my daughter, Penny Pocock, for their constant encouragement.

ILLUSTRATIONS

Sybil Thorndike Casson [photo: Mark Mulock], *page* 14

A page from Dame Sybil's autobiographical MS, *page* 21

Agnes Bowers, photograph taken in about 1881, *page* 28

Arthur Thorndike, photograph taken in about 1882, *page* 29

MS. of Agnes's letter dated 28 July 1881, *page* 81

MS. of Arthur's letter dated 30 July 1881, *page* 82

Bessie Bowers, Donnie's mother, *page* 136

Donnie Thorndike and Sybil, 1882, *page* 141

Canon and Mrs Arthur Thorndike with Sybil, Eileen and Frank, April 1897, *page* 153

Donnie Thorndike, photograph taken in about 1925, *page* 158

*To our grandson
Randal Casson,
the great-great-grandson
of Arthur and Donnie*

INTRODUCTION

by Patricia Casson

My mother-in-law, Dame Sybil Thorndike, died on June 9th 1976 in her 94th year. She had been determined to live longer than her husband, Lewis Casson, and three weeks after achieving this, she slipped away peacefully. The lights dimmed for a vast public round the world, not least for her family and certainly for me personally. We were devoted friends over forty years and I loved her. Over those years she would often say, 'I suppose I shall have to write a book one day about my life. It's been such fun and I have so many wonderful memories – but oh! there never seems to be time.' And there never was.

When she died, a trunk load of family papers arrived in our house to be sorted and browsed over in a more leisurely moment. It took five years for that moment to come. One day rather to my surprise, I found I had some spare time and so brought down the trunk. Within minutes I was surrounded by a mountain of papers and letters. Sybil wrote prolifically to everyone and kept everyone's letters to her. Amongst this sea of correspondence, essays and papers I found a large envelope containing pages of her writing in a rather sprawling hand. I started to read avidly. It was her first attempt at a book and she had started with a flourish, 'It is my 60th birthday so I am beginning my book . . .' I read on, fascinated by her racy enthusiasm, but alas, her 'book' did not last for long and came to an abrupt end. Perhaps she had been doing a great tour with a play or recitals with Lewis in India, Australia, Africa or America, and enjoying it all far more than writing! I went on rummaging through the trunk and came upon a large, red, marbled hard-backed exercise book. There on the first page was the same sprawling hand and the same flourishing style but saying, this time, 'It is my 65th birthday so I am beginning my book . . .' This version lasted longer than the first but again her story petered out. However not before she had written about her parents and their early life.

I returned to the mass of papers in the trunk and, with mounting excitement, at the very bottom I came upon an old leather-bound notebook with a lock, presumably to guard something precious from prying eyes, and a bundle of letters tied together with faded pink ribbon. The notebook and the bundle contained the letters between Sybil's father, Arthur Thorndike, and his beloved wife, Agnes, during their engagement just over one hundred years ago. I started to read and found myself transported into another world. A slower world, a world where letters were written daily and where there were four or five postal deliveries daily; a world where people understood their absolute values, and words like romance and love meant a great deal more than a transient song.

In her own notebook Sybil had written about her parents, their background and their early life with such humour and charm that I felt there could be no better way of making her fragment of autobiography public than by using it to introduce her parents' letters, which are in turn the natural sequel to her notebook.

At first, as I started to read the letters of Arthur and Agnes I found it somewhat puzzling that they would write parts of their letters in the third person as though someone else was there too, and often, in the middle of a letter, change from 'I' to 'He' or 'Her'. However it wasn't long before I accepted this rather endearing idiosyncrasy, and hardly noticed the changes. Inevitably, as I tried to fit the letters together chronologically, I found there were some missing, mainly from Agnes, whose letters had been bound into the locked notebook, during the month of August 1881. Whether someone had removed them we shall never know but with Arthur's letters virtually intact it is perfectly easy to guess at Agnes's replies and to imagine her robust views on life and marriage! It is somewhat puzzling that often Agnes did not sign her letters and engaging that her spelling was at times somewhat shaky. But Arthur had no trouble at all in signing his letters, in a different form for almost every letter. After they were married Arthur immediately adopted Agnes's family nickname of 'Donnie',* varying this with 'Dear Old Thing' and 'My Own Wifie'. Owing to the speed and number of postal deliveries and the fact that they were writing simultaneously every day, at times their letters overlapped but it does not appear to make for any serious confusion.

As well as Arthur's and Agnes's letters I have included a few of Agnes's mother's letters to illustrate how much she helped the young couple during their early years of marriage, for there was no doubt that Agnes and Arthur would have found life very hard if Bessie Bowers had not helped them, particularly during the months before Sybil was born. The hampers that arrived regularly from Southampton must have been a godsend and were certainly greatly appreciated.

The decision to publish these letters, taken jointly by me and my husband, John Casson, Sybil's son, is not so that we may all become Peeping Toms into the charming romance of two young people very much in love, but rather that we may have a glimpse of a corner of English life that was more stable, more patterned and perhaps more formal than our own. They were, of course, private letters and as such they are totally sincere, though perhaps not entirely unselfconscious as is the way with young lovers. Arthur and Donnie were in love with an absolute faith, first and foremost in each other, but also in the stability of their English world, in the Church of England, of which Arthur was a minister, and in their God from whom all their oft-counted blessings flowed.

---

* Agnes was christened Agnes Macdonald Bowers and in the family she was always 'Don' or 'Donnie', also adopted by Arthur after they married. Her grandchildren all called her Granny Don Don.

The Beginnings of an

AUTOBIOGRAPHY

by Sybil Thorndike Casson

It is my 65th birthday, so I am beginning my book. Some years ago I said to myself, 'When I am 65 I will write a book.' It was Benvenuto Cellini who first put the idea in my head – not that I have any great respect for him, but this was one of his good ideas. 'Everyone,' he said, 'should write one book, a record of a life must always hold the interest – there is no life that's dull, no life without some sign of growth, and a thing grown or growing holds in it some excitement.' The book may be perhaps for no one but myself, for in the writing of it there is a tidying up of my inner affairs: it is a way of becoming aware, and since all life is a growing awareness – awakeness – this writing of a book of one's life is an aid – a sort of confession – then, leave it behind or use it and tidy it away, and go on to the next thing! So I will start at the beginning, and the beginning goes back so far, to one's parents, to one's grand-parents, and so lucky that we cannot remember further back or we'd never have done with heredity.

I was born on October 24th 1882 in the town of Gainsborough, Lincolnshire: always I was annoyed that I had not first seen the light in the cathedral city of Rochester, where my brothers and sister were born. It seemed all wrong somehow when the Cathedral was my whole childhood, and my brother, Russell, would always crow over me because Father was only at an ordinary parish church as a curate for my birth, whereas he had become a minor canon for Russell's entry – and a minor canon was a more dignified father to have. However, Gainsborough it was, and curate it was, and maybe it accounts for my innate love of the northern counties and curates.

One must begin with one's parents. Always it is one's parents' fault when one makes errors, when one does something more than usually foolish, and when one achieves something worthwhile it is because of one's *own* strivings and strugglings and character – so do we bolster up ourselves.

My father was the son of one Daniel Thorndike – a general in the Royal Artillery – a keen soldier who had never seen active service but was proud of his military career, and I fancy a bit proud of his success as an amateur actor and performer on the flute. He [Daniel] had married a very beautiful young woman, who gave him a son and daughter, and when they were still almost babies, and while Daniel Thorndike was in church one fine Sunday morning, took herself off with a less religious and more dashing young man. This was a terrible blow to the General (what his rank was then I do not know) who was as proud of his respectability as he was of his acting and flute playing. Never was the erring wife's name mentioned again, and in spite of his strict religion, he divorced her and she was as dead. I believe her children never heard of her again.

After a long while Daniel married again, a much younger woman than himself. She was Isabella Russell who completely fitted into his scheme of life, being vivacious, religious and obedient and she played the piano – not very well, I imagine, according to the story we always heard as children of her 'Prince Albert March' played for young folk at a party and the General saying, 'You're playing the wrong notes Isabella,' to which she cheerfully replied, 'But never mind, they're dancing to it, Papa.' Five children she had: Godfrey and Russell, both dying when young, Arthur John Webster who was my father, Francis and Isabella. Francis chose the army, and much as my father would have liked to be a soldier, he was not allowed to have a say in the matter – the church for him. Being very religious from a small boy, as were all the family, this didn't worry him at all – soldier of England and soldier of Christ being one and the same thing!

The atmosphere of their home was that of a godly Victorian household – morning and evening prayers with the whole family and servants and reading of Scriptures by the General. His sonorous mouthed diction, which all the Thorndikes seemed to have, was most impressive. The son and daughter of the first marriage were almost old enough to be parents of the younger family. The eldest, Charles, was in the army, and later became ordained and had the same beautiful voice and diction which was passed on to his large family, all of whom were singers, Herbert Thorndike and Emily Thorndike (afterwards Hart-Dyke) being the only two to achieve distinction as professionals. The daughter, Julia, had the same deep contralto voice – she married one Charles Duppa and I can still hear her vibrating voice when I recall staying with her during the Boer War: and she prayed each morning at family prayers for every general as if he were her dearest, and trembling with emotion she would finish with 'and one poor General Buller and not forgetting General Gatacre' – this last name in a sort of compassionate whisper: I was thrilled when we got to Gatacre, for the smell of bacon coffee and eggs was beyond bearing and the cook always began to shuffle when Buller came on. That particular quality of voice, however, persisted thro' all the family: they all sang most dramatically and with tremendous emotion, my own father included, the drama just a bit overdone in every case.

Father was a very ordinary boy, no particular brilliance, but with an imaginative mystic religious sense and a passion for rowing and tennis. At St John's, Cambridge, he rowed for his college and missed being in the Cambridge crew for the great Holy Week race by being a few pounds under weight. He did quite well in whatever he undertook in studies and sport because he had a tremendous zest in life, and thoroughly enjoyed mastering difficulties whether it was Latin prose or making cigar boxes into chests of drawers. His carpentering feats, which were considerable, always annoyed my mother because she said, 'Your father enjoys making silly little three-legged stools and useless nonsense – he hasn't any ambition to get to the top of the tree.' Before ordination he became a lay reader in Bere Regis, Dorset, and Thomas Hardy told one of my family that he remembered a 'beautiful fair-haired lay reader who used to be in and out of the cottages with great diligence and persistence, his Bible under his arm – and his name was Thorndike.' While at Cambridge his best friend was John Allcot Bowers, whose sister Agnes came a-visiting. She was a first class pianist and of course accompanied Arthur Thorndike in his rendering of 'The Devout Lover', 'To Anthea', and Tosti's 'Goodbye'. She thought him rather a conceited young man because he had a habit when worked up emotionally of curling his nose midway which looked somehow supercilious!

That was my father's first meeting with my mother and she made a great impression on him. They met again a few years later when Father and his friend, John Bowers, were fellow curates at St Mary's, Redcliffe – Bristol. Characteristic of my mother was this meeting. A festive procession – my mother in the church with her brother's wife – and as the choir passed their pew going up the aisle singing 'Onward Christian Soldiers' my mother whispered to her sister-in-law, 'Louie, I could marry that man who is walking with Jack.' His hair had gone darker and she hadn't recognised him but her mind was made up and two weeks later they were engaged – my mother's tact again, for on being asked by Arthur T. how much two people could live on, she deducted half the income she knew he had and answered to his joy: so all was fixed up and they were married in three months' time.

Now Mother's family were very different. Grandfather John Bowers, with Macdonald tacked on somewhere, lived in Elgin in north Scotland. His people were the postmen of the then little town and one of my grandfather's duties, apart from the post office, was to watch the sheep in the surrounding meadows. It was here that he taught himself mathematics and educated himself by reading while the silly sheep wandered round and about. He was a quiet ambitious boy and worried his father till he was allowed to apprentice himself to an engineering shop in Aberdeen. One day, hearing two men say they'd give twenty pounds to anyone who could find the flaw in a certain machine and set

far — to ones parents — to ones grand parents
so many that we cannot remember
further back & we'd never have done
with heredity — I was born Oct 24
1882 in the town of Gainsborough
Lincolnshire — always was annoyed
that I had not first seen the light in
the Cathedral City of Rochester when the
my brother & sister were born —
it seemed all wrong somehow when the
Cathedral was my whole childhood; &
my brother Russell would always crow
over me because Father was only at an
ordinary parish church as a curate
for my birth whereas he had become a
minor Canon & a minor Canon was a more
dignified father to have — However Gainsborough
I was & curate it was & maybe it accounts
for my innate love of the northern counties scenery

A page from Dame Sybil's autobiographical MS.

it to rights, young John Bowers hopped up and said he'd do it. He got the £20 and immediately shipped himself as an apprentice on one of the boats going to Southampton, where he somehow squirmed himself into the Royal Mail Line and finished his career as Consulting Engineer of the Union Castle Line. He married Betsy Allcot, a Hampshire girl living at Porchester: they had three sons and three daughters, John, William and Ted, Adela Fanny, Agnes Macdonald (my mother) and Belle, the youngest. The sons all became parsons; Jack, my uncle, was the eldest and the only one who achieved distinction; he became a canon, then Archdeacon of Gloucester and then Bishop of Thetford and I believe has the unique distinction of being the only bishop whose memorial likeness is a laughing one. The plaque in the choir of Norwich Cathedral portrays his jolly face with a broad grin. I am told that he had cheered so many people with his funny stories even in the pulpit that it was impossible to have a solemn memorial of him. The other two sons were a bit wild; both had brilliant careers at Oxford but they should have been actors not parsons. The youngest, Uncle Ted, got himself into such difficulties with his goings on that his father paid his debts and gave him a sum of money and packed him off to America where luckily he married a charming Canadian girl and finished up a dignitary of the Episcopal Church in Texas. The middle brother – Uncle Willie – was something of a genius but wasted in the church. He had terrible ups and downs – a splendid wife and a gift of making money, gambling on the stock exchange which was his main amusement. If he wanted anything new for his church or parish he'd go and have a fling and a gamble and come back with the ready money for new candlesticks for the altar. He was a wildly exciting if over-theatrical preacher. His church in Gillingham in Kent used to be packed to the doors with dockyard men; it was a sight I'll never forget – a thing we seldom see now – a whole congregation in a state of emotion, tears pouring down their faces and with his dramatic performance making them laugh or cry as he willed. In the vestry afterwards he'd catch hold of one and say, 'Well, how did it go –

I got 'em didn't I – not a dry eye in the place.' I used to think it humbugging and so did Father but it wasn't – it was drama – it was a stage performance.

Mother also had a wild streak like Uncle Willy but she was strongly religious too and used to play the organ for church and have Sunday School classes – but they were very unorthodox, I'm quite sure. She sang and played with such ease and naturalness and I think she provided my father with a gaiety and a sense of the ridiculous which saved him from being the complete religious. They were tremendously in love – always to the end – a very happy marriage of two people who couldn't have been more unlike. They were married in September 1881 and went to Barley, near Royston, Cambridgeshire for their first curacy. Mother said she saved £100 the first year out of his £250 stipend. Well, if she did it was the first time she'd ever saved a penny, for she slid gaily downhill in the money way for ever after! They moved to a senior curateship of the parish church of Gainsborough just in time for me to be born on October 24th 1882. I say 'they' in the plural moved to the curateship, for Mother really did share the work of the church with Father and brought to all their efforts her ridiculous sense of fun and exuberant high spirits, which made the church life for us exciting with never a dull moment.

I find now I'm old such joy in going over the doings of the generations that have gone and finding their thoughts and actions reflected and re-lived in my own life and my children. Heredity is an absorbing study – our forebears live in us and bear their part in all we do. This gives me a fresh zest for living when I look at my own grandchildren and see the thrill of life which was, in that older generation, reflected again in them.

1947

THE LETTERS

of Agnes Bowers and Arthur Thorndike

Glen Luie
Lower Avenue
Southampton
4 June 1881

My Very Dear Arthur,

My hand shakes so that I can hardly write. I suppose the reason is because it is my first love letter to you.

I found the luggage quite safely; the guard was most attentive; my cousin and Auntie met me at Southampton. Amy, James, Bella and Bertha Thring, my greatest friend who is staying here, had all gone to the theatre. Papa was in town all day; I came home about five o'clock, so dear Mother and myself had a good chat over things. Several gentlemen came home with the girls from the theatre and I received no end of congratulations. Fred Wilde is here for a day or two and I think will soon be engaged to Bertha. I have been promised heaps of presents already.

Now dear, to business. James has nothing whatever to do on Tuesday and has made up his mind for a jolly trip to the Island in the steam launch, so that if possible, dear, do come on Monday, or early on Tuesday, but don't let this interfere with Royston at all. I am longing to see you, darling. Papa sobbed bitterly last night, he said he felt so thankful I should have a good husband, he was so sweet, and is going to give me everything he can. I never went to bed until one o'clock, but did not forget my reading. I thought of you and of course you came often in my prayers. Oh, Arthur I will try to be a good wife, and strive to be loved by our people. I hope you will like Royston; I dreamt about that

Agnes Bowers, c. 1881

myricle – I know I haven't spelt it correctly, she is such an ignorant child. Today Bella, Bertha and Fred Wilde are going to Southsea, to hear the band. I shall be working hard, dear, and my thoughts you know where. Mary (our housemaid) is such a nice girl and not expensive, I should like to have her with us, she knows her work thoroughly and quite understands me; she is longing to see you, everything looks so bright I feel so happy. I woke up at six o'clock, the birds were singing in the garden and Donnie's heart was lighter than any bird's. I do feel thankful for all these blessings and pray that my life may be an unselfish one. Now, darling, I must catch the post. Come in time for the trip on Tuesday if possible.

Fondest love and kisses from your very own,
AGNES

Arthur Thorndike, c. 1882

The Paragon
Bath
6 June 1881

Dear One,

He must just write her a line before going to roost to tell her that
she has been in his thoughts today, especially at the 7 o'clock
celebrations. The Mayor and Corporation made a grand display
with their scarlet robes and bouquets. I have such a bad pen. He
did like her dear letter so much, especially when she said in that
way he loves so that she was happier than the birds. Oh, dear
one, he does love her so and he tries to be very thankful that
God has provided him with such a loving one as she is. He cannot
say for certain about what time he will be able to arrive at
Southampton. If he cannot see all about Barley by the next train
tomorrow night he will come on by the early one Tuesday

morning. She does not say when they start for the Island. I hope to be able to see about the trains from Barley to Southampton before posting this: He leaves here tomorrow at 8.7 and gets to Royston at 1.10. Dear, he must get to bed, so wishing her goodnight and sending her his very best love.

> He still, and forever, remains her loving,
> ARTHUR

Leave Royston 6.30 Monday
Leave Waterloo 8.00 Tuesday
Arrive Southampton 11.3

Glen Luie, 10 June 1881

My Own Dear Arthur,

After leaving you at the station I came straight home and made up my mind not to get miserable as you wished. Bella and Bertha went to St Denys' to meet you with flowers, but were just in time to see the train start – clever managers, aren't they? You will receive the flowers by post. I *do* feel jealous at their attention to you but I do trust in him so implicitly and have such perfect faith in everything he does that I would go through anything for him. I know, Arthur, that I love you as well or better than my own life. It is so sweet to think of him. She won't forget her reading every night and morning, just as he wished. You can't tell how happy I am, my heart seems brimming over with gratitude. Oh! won't I make you happy, ducky. Willie Milner has been here to tea, he is going to marry on £230 and no house, so we are better off than he is. He brought me a splendid cabinet photograph of himself for our house. I must get a frame for it. You left all your songs, shall I send them on or keep till you come. Let me know. Goodnight, darling old boy; her last thoughts will be of her own one.

> She will always be his own true,
> AGNES

30

My Dearest One,

He thinks he will write her a line while Mrs Carter is getting him something to eat to tell her that he has arrived in perfect safety. Mother and Isabella met him at the station and we had a few minutes chat. They are coming over to lunch tomorrow to hear all the news and want her to come before the 27th. He told them she would be too busy and Isabella said she would work her fingers off for you if you would come. He is going to tea with Jack to have a chat over things. Vic was delighted to see me again and shrieked to express her feelings. He hopes she is not sad and moping but is his happy and cheerful Agnes, happy in the thought that soon we shall meet again.

Oh dear one, the world does seem such a different place now to what it did before he had an Agnes of his very own: a fore-taste of what the joy of Heaven will be with his fondest love.

He is her
ARTHUR

Glen Luie, 11 June 1881

My Very Dear Arthur,

I have just given Papa his breakfast and seen him off in the car. All the others as usual are in bed. There were thirteen to supper last night; being rather superstitious, I wouldn't sit at the table, so sat in a corner at a small rush table; I had there a grand oppor-tunity for thinking, only now and then it was a great bother as they would keep appealing to me and I did so want to be quiet. Then after supper they made me go through 'The Pirates'. We landed upstairs to rest about half past twelve, but I didn't forget to read. I shall never be able to learn Romans by heart but will

31

do what I can. Dr Clapham wanted to know last night if he could be our family physician; he attends the clergy gratis, only the most attractive part of it is that he lives about 30 miles away. It was simply dreadful; he and James tried to make me feel as uncomfortable as they possibly could and said most dreadful things, but they couldn't frighten me after I had made up my mind. Now dear, I must hurry off to church or there will be no organist, so with fondest love and two or three good hugs.

from your very own
AGNES

Colston Parade, 12 June 1881

My Very Dearest One,

Just received her second dear letter: he thinks she is so good to comfort him with her letters. And so, dear Sweet, he wants to try and give her some comfort by telling her that he has decided to take Barley. He posted a letter to Mr Gordon this morning and telegraphed as he desired to say he would accept the curacy. He knows she will be delighted at this and it makes him love her for it. He does hope he has taken the right step and he believes he has because he has prayed for guidance, as she has, that he might take it. The step thus taken, dear, let us pray that it may be for our happiness and for God's honour and glory: that the new sphere of work may be blessed to us both and what our poor hands can do in the Master's Vineyard may be helped and blessed by him.

He has just finished his supper with Vic [the dog] and Polly with her two sweet letters open by his side to comfort and cheer him. He is *so* thankful, dear one, to know how truly she loves him and he can only realise it by the deep and sincere love he has for her. He feels, dear, that life would be unendurable without her to share joys and troubles, and the latter will appear but light with such an angel by his side. He will try, dear, so hard to give her a happy home and a true loving heart. If her heart is brimming over with joy what must his be when he considers what a sacrifice she will have to make in order to make him happy. Oh, dear one, words cannot express what he feels in gratitude to her for such a sacrifice on her part and for giving herself to him for his own Sweet Agnes.

He had a talk with the vicar this morning and he of course talked in his old fashioned way and gave me some very good advice. I told him I intended taking Barley. He said he thought we should get on very well there at present but when a family came and sickness, then trouble and anxiety would come and if I wished to be very prudent he would say put off being married till something better turned up! I think this would be pressing prudence too far and so, dear one, he has taken Barley. We must have faith to believe that we shall be provided for, being of 'more value than many sparrows' which have their daily food provided them. He loves her so dearly that the pang of leaving Redcliffe and all its associations are as nothing to the joy before him in his home at Barley with a 'pure' one ever attendant upon him.

Mother and Isabella came over today to lunch and went to Westbury and she was the subject of all his conversation. We were discussing what would be the prettiest dresses for the bridesmaids and we thought blue cashmere dresses with alternate flounces of lace and blue plus bodice fitting tight, with blue 'Mother Hubbard' bonnets with lace or white feathers. I think this would be very pretty indeed – I am so fond of blue (light blue, of course). They suggested the bride should have a white bonnet and a little veil over her face but I do not care about that. I like the long veil and orange blossoms.

He must now, dear, read over his sermon for tomorrow. The subject is 'The Two Dwelling Places: God's a temple, Man's a home.' (His home will be Barley).

So, dear one, wishing her goodnight and may God continue to bless her, and with his fondest love he is and ever will be her adoring

ARTHUR

33

My Own Dearest One,

As the bell is just going for evensong I cannot write, which interesting fact may not be acceptable to you. I must finish this already interesting epistle afterwards so good-bye for the present.

Dear One,

He feels quite vexed that he was unable to finish his letter to her on Saturday but he knows she will forgive him when he tells her how it was. He was behindhand with his Sunday Evensong sermon. He had worked hard at it all the morn. I did some visiting in the afternoon and came in before Evensong to write to her but could not, as you see, get very far. Then after tea I sat down to another two hours of work, intending to finish by 9 and then write to you in time for the 9.00 post when Edward Morris came in and stayed to supper, tho' I gave him the hint that I had not finished my sermon. He left at 9.15. Then I set to work again and finished my sermon at 11.30 and she knows, dear, he has no time on Sunday for writing so, dear, he hopes she will not think he is tired of writing to her, for nothing delights him more than scribbling to his sweet Agnes. Dear One, it has been a hard day's work today but still a happy one. He does not feel that depressed feeling that he used to have, for I have always a sort of notion that there is someone who takes an interest in me and often the thought comes across me it would please her if she could know I did well and then, dear, the higher thought comes: If I would do this better for her sake how much better I ought to do it for my Master's sake – so, dear, already he is opening under the warm sunshine of her love.

The service has been very nice today. Claxton and I took the 8 o'clock celebration. There were only 16 communicants but the L. Ch. always appears empty now to me lacking the one on whom my mind delights to dwell. I had to open Sunday School as Mr Francombe is away on his holiday. Mr Dickerson gave us a sermon on the epistle on the shamefulness of those things that are done in secret, i.e. the works of darkness.

The Vicar discoursed on the collect to the children in the afternoon, dividing the collect into the four addresses to God. 1. Lord of Power. 2. Lord of Might. 3. Author of all good things. 4. Giver of Sun. And into the four petitions: 1. Graft. 2. Increase. 3. Nourish. 4. Keep.

The Vicar is very nice and simple in these kind of addresses and one can always come away refreshed. I preached in the Evensong on the 2nd Lesson, 'Whom say ye that I am'. A feeling of awe came over me when I saw the vast congregation of people to whom I was to preach and I could not help feeling how impossible it would be for me to do it unless I had been sent and appointed by God for such a work, and He who has appointed me to the work does so amply help me to fulfil the duties of my office and if it were not for the weakness and infirmity of my mortal nature how much God might do thro' me to His people. I do believe He is opening a new sphere of usefulness to us, especially to me, for I am really a very selfish fellow: but having a wife to love and cherish will soon, I hope, knock this weakness on the head.

Oh, dear, how I have been chattering to you and all about myself too. The clock has just struck 11 which tells me I ought to be in bed Sunday night. He will write a more business letter tomorrow. He may hear from Barley and from Mr Barnes Monday or Tuesday.

> With love to all and with very much for her dear self,
> He remains her ever true
> ARTHUR

Glen Luie, 13 June 1881

My Own Dear Arthur,

The photos came this morning, I have kept one of each and sent on the other to you. Thank you so much, dear, for them. I think they are famous likenesses of both of us. I went to school twice yesterday and in the evening Bertha, Bella and myself went to Woolston. Charlie Owen preached and walked home with us. He did like you so much and still wants you to accept his curacy; he says he thinks it a sin for two young people with our talent to bury ourselves in the country. I have promised to do most of the music at his temperance meeting on the 28th; be sure to come, won't you? Do you mind sending me the A.B.L. duett, then I can learn it perfectly by the time you come, and any other duett you like – I am writing so disgracefully, do excuse it like a good old thing.

Bertha, Bella are just off to Cowes for bathing. I am going into the town with Mother. You would roar with laughter at the girls, they are full of the wedding and have decided on the bridesmaids' dresses – white as you wished, white corded silk dresses, very short with lace frills shewing below, high white satin boots, very large spanish lace hats with white feathers, and baskets of crimson flowers. Won't they outshine the plump and pleasing bride? I cannot see how I am to come to Bath, for I feel full of business and am deep in the subject of cheesecakes, satisfaction, etc. I had a jolly letter from Mrs Taylor. She did write so sweetly and told me I should be her future aunt. Have you heard from Barley since? Any news about the furniture, dear? Bertha is going to work us a mantel border, passion flowers on ruby satin ground. Oh! Arthur, I do feel so happy. I did think of him all day yesterday, and longed to catch a glimpse of his darling face – she does love him so dearly, he is the one man in the world to her. She only hopes she will never grieve him, though she is a wayward child at times; with such an important thing as a husband to look after her she will be sure to improve.

With fondest love, she always remains his own true
AGNES

My Own One,

She has been in his thoughts all day, though he has not had a moment to sit down quietly and write to her before this. He is now sitting at his table with her dear face in front of him looking so happy and he feels the same, dear, with an earnest longing to press her to his heart again. Absence seems to deepen his love for her, for he feels how void life would be without her, dear one. Oh, how happy shall we be in our little home at Barley. She must have got his letter by this time pronouncing the news which he believes will be good news to her that he has accepted Barley. I got a letter from Mr Gordon this morning in answer to my telegram saying that he was delighted to find I had decided to come to work with him. He will be happy wherever his Agnes is. He has been working this afternoon for the School Treat and has collected £1.10. I have to get £36 before I come to see you on the 27th so I must look sharp about it.

Fancy allowing him to leave all his songs behind; what a thoughtful wife she will make. He knows how it was all her fault. He put them on the bed and then she turned the coverlet over them to hide them on purpose that she might keep something of his and prevent him from taking Bella's photo. Oh! what a designer she is. If that is the way she is going to treat him when she is his wife, he will have to keep his eyes about him; he feels he has given her quite a scolding when he is the one to blame all the time. She had better keep his songs now, as well as his racquet, till he comes.

The services were very nice yesterday, dear, tho' they lacked the bodily presence of the one he loves dearer than anything on earth. He thought of her all day especially in the H.C. He went to Cripps' in the evening and had to shut up Cripps for referring to you as 'my girl', vulgar fellow. I said, 'I suppose you mean Miss Bowers' and he did not use that vulgar term towards you again. Mrs Norris was very nice to me today and expressed her great sorrow at the thought of losing me. It will be a great pang to leave here but, dear one, he would go thro' fifty times worse things for her dear sake, and she also will have great, much greater, pangs than his at leaving her home and those she loves and he hopes she will have strength given her to bear them. My time, dear, will be up about the 11th September. Will she think over the matter and name the Day when he is to be made the happiest man in the world? Would it be better to be married the week after he leaves here, then spend a few days in London or wherever she likes and *then* go to Barley, or, for him to go to Barley and get things a little into shape and spend a Sunday there to get a little accustomed to the work and people and *then* be married and bring her down to his home?

The Vicar said the other day, 'If you could guarantee not to have a family, you could live very comfortably but when babies come and fall sick and your wife gets ill in consequence, then your troubles begin.' Many people have struck the same nail on the head, that the family causes the distress. Well, dear, he could be perfectly happy with her without the family, then we need not fear for money to educate them, etc. Dear One, she won't mind him talking in this matter-of-fact way, but if we come to such a determination three months is not a bit too long a time to gain strength to carry out such a determination. He begs her pardon for having broached this delicate subject and hopes she will forgive him.

What does she think about the blue cashmere dresses; he fancies all white would be very trying for the bridesmaids, tho' the idea is very nice. Would not those large hats rather bury Isabella and Bella? Would 'Mother Hubbard' bonnets look well?

I have just had a letter from Mother about Elizabeth, the maid whom Mother thinks would be invaluable. He sends it to her — will she write back an answer soon about her. It is very good of Mother to fit her out so well. I don't think we can do better than take her for 1/6 and raise her wages each year.

I proposed to Mother that she should take a trip to the Isle of Wight as we are not going to the Lakes. Could you give me any idea how much lodgings are in Ventnor?

Good night, dear one. He longs for the 27th.

> With his fondest love, he is her own
> ARTHUR

My Own Darling Arthur,

I was delighted with your sweet letter yesterday: it seems quite like a dream to me that we are really going to be married so soon; I don't think I shall quite realize it even when we are married, but I do feel so thankful it is all settled, and I do think, dear, you have taken the right step. You talk about the sacrifice I am making; I think the sacrifice is all on your side; you are in fact giving up everything for me and I do pray, darling, that I may some day be able to repay you for all this goodness to me who has done so little to deserve it. I have just written to Mrs Thorndike and explained everything. Of course I must not be selfish, and want you quite to myself for the week, but you will stay in our house, won't you, dear, and have the same room as you had before? I will get one sitting room and bedroom for Mrs Thorndike and Isabella. Papa is very sorry he cannot take them in as well but you know the house is not large enough, and Mother's head is still so weak that she is quite unable to entertain as she would wish, but I think, Arthur dear, we shall all be very happy together. Do you think they would like to go in the steam launch one day? Bertha will be here so we shall be a very jolly party. I want you to explain, dear, how you are going to arrange. After that week will you stay on with me a little longer or will your Mother want you with her? It will be dreadful to part again, I don't know how I shall be able to see you go away. It was almost more than I could bear the last time, but of course, Arthur, I mustn't dictate to you, as I am so soon to obey, but if possible you will be as much as you can with me, won't you?

I wish, dear, we could arrange about the wedding (of course

I don't mean the date) but do you think you will be ready the beginning of September? Of course I shall be ready when you want me and could manage it before then very well if you wished. Have you heard about the furniture? Of course you will tell me when you know. Oh! Arthur what a sight I should look in a bonnet and veil. I wouldn't, darling, appear in such a thing. My dress will be a rich ivory white satin, with very long veil and a wreath of orange blossom. I have written to Isabella about the bridesmaids' dresses. All the little weddings about here the girls always wear pale blue or pink, so we shall be quite out of the common, and the dresses will look so handsome and so pure, and I think marrying a clergyman I ought to study this. The baskets of dark crimson flowers will give a splendid effect to the white silk dresses, quite short with lace frills – don't laugh, dear, but these little things must be arranged. I should write to my brother if I were you and ask him about the groomsmen; also to your other friends, so that if they are unable to come we can provide others in their place. I do feel so happy, darling, yet of course at the same time I feel anxious. I do think we are everything to each other now, but on that day Arthur I shall feel most sacred, I know I shall; don't be nervous, dear, will you or perhaps in a weak moment I may break down, but I hope not. After all the goodbyes I shall have a splitting headache but how lovely it will be to think we shall be together and nothing on earth can separate us. She will be able to look up to him so, and ask his advice about everything. I will work hard to get loved by your people and try and help him all she can in his work. Now, dearest Arthur, I hope to hear soon. I can hardly wait for the time to come – she wishes she possessed half his patience and half his goodness – she will try so hard to be better.

> Fondest love,
> She is always his own
> AGNES

My Very Own Arthur,

I have just received your letter, and if you will take me, dear, let me come to Barley with you and commence our work together; I shall be quite ready any day after the 11th, as soon as you like, and if we have about two or three days in London I shall be only too glad to get to Barley. We shall soon feel at home. I didn't mind you talking to me about the family but, Arthur dear, I am afraid I have been very naughty expressing my opinion so freely; we must leave all these little things in other hands and take things as they come. Seriously, I know we shall be happier with a family than without one and I should be very disappointed if I thought I should never be a mother. A child brings the most sacred love with it and is such a tie between husband and wife. Don't get down in the dumps about me, darling, as I am very strong and would go through any amount of pain or trouble for him; perhaps I ought not to have said all this, dear, but I feel that I am almost talking to my husband, and I thought it all, so wanted to tell him and unburden her mind; she does love him so and he mustn't fancy and imagine all these little troubles. Look what a broad back she has and if broad enough to play tennis, surely it will do to give her husband and the terrible little family (he is so afraid of) a pig-a-back, when they feel fatigued. Don't laugh, duckey, and think I am frivelling because I mean all I say and I know I shall be one of the happiest wives and (I hope) mothers in England. I shall never make a trouble, and always try to look on the bright side of things; I think two people loving each other as we do, and with contented minds, is far better than all the riches in the world; we couldn't take them with us. I shall value the life I am to lead most highly. Do write and give me a wee bit of comfort, dear. She fancied he was low spirited by his letter; and do, Arthur, take me with you, won't you?

Goodnight darling, Ever your fond and loving
AGNES

My Own Dearest One,

Received her sweet letter this morning. Jack came to breakfast and we chatted over the wedding. She must do what she likes about the dresses, dear. He likes the idea of representing her maids as Purity as her own name signifies. Will she, dear one, write to Dora Evans and ask her to be one of your maids. She will like it so much. She said she *would* come to the wedding to see me married having known me for such a long time. It would come very gracefully if she would write and ask her. Has she decided upon seven bridesmaids. If so, there must be seven groomsmen? My brother, your two brothers, Jendwine, Layard, my cousin the singist and I can ask my brother to bring one of his brother officers.

About the time of the wedding. To my mind it will fit best this way. My time will be up as curate of Redcliffe on September 11th which is Sunday. I might make the 4th the last. Then I would go to Barley for a few days to see things were straight, come to Southampton in that same week, be married on Thursday the 8th. Get off Sunday duty on the 11th, spend a few days holiday somewhere and return to Barley for our first Sunday duty on the 18th. What does she think of this arrangement?

Now about his holiday. He has given up one week, as his time is so short at Redcliffe and I think the Vicar likes my having done it. The first week she says he is to spend with her – she thinks of course he will like that. He supposes he must give in to her on this point. Then, dear, it depends very much on what Mother and Isabella intend doing. I feel they want some good bracing sea air which I do not think they would get at Southampton. I have not heard whether Mother has decided to go to S'hampton but he supposes she has so he thinks a trip to the Isle of Wight would be beneficial for them and he would go too and she would come over in the launch and we should see as much of each other as possible. Then he would return to Redcliffe and set his district in order and put his house out of order by packing, etc. Mother and Isabella are not very fond of the water but they might like to go in the launch.

I have not heard anything about the furniture yet. The bonnet for her was only a suggestion and he is glad she hates it as much as he would.

He nearly knows the last chapter of Romans by heart. Two fresh verses a day soon gets thro' a chapter. How does she get on, dear?

> With his fondest love to his 'Pure One',
> He remains her own
> ARTHUR

Colston Parade, 15 June 1881

My One,

Must just write her a line to go by the evening post. He likes the photos very much. She looks a darling. He has put her in the frame she gave him and has placed it on his desk in front of him so that whenever he reads or writes he has her before him to cheer him. He thinks, dear, somehow or other, can't imagine how, that she is very sweet.

What does she think about taking Elizabeth? Mother will take her at once and begin training her if we decide to take her. She, being the house manager, must decide. Mother thinks she will be as good as two – can turn her hand to anything and hopes we shall keep her at Sunday School. I suppose you will have to take the girls' class so Elizabeth would be under your eye.

He must stop writing, dear, and get to some sermon work.

> He remains
> Her ARTHUR

My Own Arthur,

I am so sorry you will not get this by the first post but I will confess to you, dear, Papa went to Town by the early train this morning so we all took advantage of it and were rather lazy. I am so sorry and hope you will forgive me. Of course it was all fun on my part about Mr Owen, I wouldn't accept his curacy for the world. I would much rather be at Redcliffe but of course Arthur, dear, I think we have done wisely. Barley seems to have come to us just at the right time and you are always free to go in for anything better. I am charmed with the idea, and think we shall have a perfect home; if we had to pay house rent out of our income we should find it rather hard work. She fancies it will grieve him dreadfully giving up Redcliffe all for her. Does he feel very sad at the thought? She will try and comfort him so and study him in everything; he mustn't get low-spirited for we shall be perfectly happy.

Now darling, about the dresses. After your first suggestion we talked it over and all the bridesmaids here jumped with delight at the idea; we shall not have a blue white, but ivory white; it is most becoming and as our church is very dark, will have a much better effect than the blue. I think blue cashmere dresses most ordinary. I don't think at any of the weddings here there has ever been any other colour. At all the very small ones the girls all sport pale blue so that it is quite hackneyed. Our dresses will be made in a very old fashioned original style, with puffings of lace in the sleeves and lace frills to show below the skirts. I am sure you will be charmed with the effect when you see them; we have a splendid dressmaker, and she has just brought over the latest from Paris. She quite laughed at the idea of our wearing blue; so you see, darling old sweet, what am I to do? I can't please everybody – of course I want to please him as much as I can. I shall have a pale blue dress in my trousseau, as he likes the colour so much – but let us keep the wedding dresses as decided, they are lovely and so are the hats. Bella says much as she likes

you, neither Bertha or herself would wear a granny bonnet.
Now, darling, tell your old Agnes how to act, she is anxious for
an answer to her last letter and hopes he wasn't angry.

She is always his own dear one.

Beloved One,

He is going to try and give his Agnes the wee bit of comfort she
desires. He thinks he paid her out very well for poking fun at
him about Mr Owen. He quite took her in and made her think
he was in earnest about giving up Barley. He would not give it
up for anything provided she will come with him; without her
life would be miserable now. It will be somewhat hard to leave
Redcliffe and all its associations, but, dear, when he looks at what
he is gaining by the move, all his regrets vanish. Oh, dearest
Agnes, I do think we shall be very happy together, for he loves
her so intensely, better than he has ever loved anybody in his
life before and he believes she loves him which makes him so
happy. He leaves the arrangement of the dresses entirely, dear,
with her and feels confident that her choice will be the prettiest,
he is quite prepared to be charmed with the white. He would not
wish the dresses to be like the common herd, but something good,
tasteful and ladylike. Has she written to Dora Evans, dear? He
would like her to be á bridesmaid.

About the nine children*, dear, he cannot decide anything but
rather dreads such a lot. He will take a lesson from her, sweet one,
and leave this matter in God's hands and pray that he will not be
led into lustful excesses. He quite talks to her as if she were his

---

* Sadly, Agnes's letter suggesting nine children is missing and we shall
never know whether Arthur may have deleted it in embarrassment or
whether someone else removed it. Whatever the reason, it is clear that
Agnes's original enthusiasm for a very large family may have waned, for
they only had four children and that appeared to be enough.

wife, therefore this feeling is mutual. He hopes the same will exist in all other matters in our married life. He does not feel he has answered her anxious questions about the family. He thinks nine is a lucky number and we could give them all names beginning with A, it would be such a pretty token. The five boys we could name – Artemas, Arcturus, Alfred, Arthur, Albert and the four girls – Agnes, Armidallah (such a sweet name), Achsah (still prettier) and youngest Aholibamah. What a tribe we shall have. I hope you like the names: make a note of them or say if you would like any alteration: perhaps it might be confusing to have two children with our own names, therefore I would suggest instead of Agnes, Asaiah, and instead of Arthur, Adombezek, as he was a king and it would be nice to have our firstborn named after a king.

He is going to take duty for the Rev. Medd, somewhere the other side of Gloucester on Sunday week, as that Rev. gentleman is coming here. I shall have to go on Saturday so she must write to him there.

Off to ring for service,

> His fondest love to his ever beloved Agnes,
> ARTHUR

Glen Luie, 16 June 1881

My Very Dear Arthur,

Just received your letter and quite agree with everything you say. It would be very charming for you to go to the Island, as I could easily come to you there, but if you go to a strange place, I should most awfully like to come with you all and of course pay my own expenses; if you are only in the Island, of course I could come over often from here. I think that the time for the wedding would suit very well; we will have it that week. Do you mind my leaving the exact date for a few days, as when once decided cannot alter and there are several little things to be considered, but I am almost sure that the time will suit. Now, dear, to another subject, would it be quite etiquette for Canon Norris to come without tying the knot himself? Of course I wish my own Vicar to marry me and give the address; he would be more than grieved not to do so. I shall leave it to his own judgement as he understands these little matters better than she does. Now about Dora. I am going to write and ask her if she will be one of the guests, as the bridesmaids are all decided; we mustn't have an even number; there are seven already of my oldest girl friends with Isabella, so that I think she will be just as pleased to come as a guest; I shall make it quite plain to her and write a nice letter.

I had a letter from your mother this morning and am going to find lodgings for them. I wrote to her about Elizabeth and decided to have her. I will see about a cook; if we give £10 a year, Mother says she will make up the wages to £15, as she wouldn't like me to have a servant who couldn't do things very nicely for us; it is really more economical as a good servant can always make little dishes out of things which an inferior servant might not understand, so it is very good of both our mothers to help us as they are. We can choose our own piano when we are in town at Collards' warehouse; my music master will meet us there, his brother is manager at Collards' so he will get all the commission off; that is one of Papa's presents. I think now I have told you everything. I went to a bazaar yesterday, played for an hour, had such a jolly tea-cosy given me and Willie Milner bought me a muslin child's pinafore, wasn't it cheeky of him. I am anxiously awaiting an answer to my last letter; don't be angry, Arthur dear, will you, for talking to you as I did?

Fondest love
from His Own Dear
AGNES

Where shall we put the parrot, dear?

My Own Arthur,

I waited for a letter by the first post this morning but was disappointed, suppose I shall get one by the midday post. I am so afraid you are angry with me; I really commence to think I oughtn't to have said what I did, but it was so lovely to tell you what I thought, so you will forgive the naughty girl, won't you? I wrote to Dora Evans yesterday, also to your mother about lodgings. It was quite as good as a play to see Bertha and myself enquiring at every house where we saw apartments in the window. I am looking forward to the 27th, fancy your being here with me again. We are all to spend one day in Winchester with Mrs Thring and in the afternoon go down to the tennis club; you must play with some of the men there, then you will get some decent games. Bertha is going home on Tuesday and coming back on the 27th. If you will let me know what time you will come, you can all meet at Bishopstoke; you will not have to change, but Bertha will soon see you. Perhaps Willie will be home from Oxford, I hope he will.

Now, Arthur dear, I do love your letters so, they quite keep my spirits up; the days seem like years now you are away. Don't I long to have another peep at you; and I haven't said 'beastly' since you left, so she will improve in time and be so refined when she is his own. Goodbye Darling, you are always in the thoughts

Of Your Very Own
AGNES

Colston Parade, 17 June 1881

My Very Dearest One,

He cannot let the day pass away without writing her a few words. He has been so busy all day and is now just out from service having preached on the Surety of God's promise, especially pressing Ps. 37, 3 & 4. But there was no Donnie to play the harmonium – only fat Mrs Biggs. He often sees her in the Lady Chapel in his mind's eye and it always gives him delight, therefore what will he feel when he sees her in reality. Oh, what happiness, dear, too deep to realize.

Now business, dear. It is very good of your mother to give us £5 a year towards a servant. It will be most acceptable but, dear one, he does not think it will be wise to get a *cook* or to give her £15 a year. She will be always giving herself airs and will not turn her hand to anything but cooking. Now, this is not the sort of servant we shall want. The most useful one would be a good general servant who could turn her hand to anything and today I saw an advertisement of one that looks promising. The advertisement is 'General Servant in small family, aged 23 willing and useful, communicant, London objected to. Address Miss Wells, St Peter's Street, Winchester.' I think it is worth writing about. You might be able to see her. Offer her a place in clergyman's house – pretty country village, 3 miles from Royston, 1½ hours from London. Salary £7 all found and I believe she would jump at it. Will you write to her or see her and let me know. I might be able to pick up a good general servant in my last Parish. Mrs Norris would help me but see first if this one will do. Jack thinks with me that she would. He must close now or miss the post.

His fondest love to his own darling Agnes,
From her ever true
ARTHUR

Loui wants her Mizpah ring.

Glen Luie, 18 June 1881

My Own Dear Arthur,

You ridiculous old darling! How could you be so absurd, your letter has given me no end of comfort for he did not seem in a low-spirited way when he wrote it. Do take care of yourself, don't work too hard and if you ever feel weak or ill be sure and tell me at once or I will never forgive you. About the girls' names, dear! With the select ones you have chosen, we shall never get them married, and one of our principal aims must be to prevent expense; any man would tremble to approach them, so that when we get aged, we shall want a little quiet and not wish to be surrounded by 5 Miss Thorndikes. I can see them with the eye of imagination walking one by one; don't you think then that there must be some alteration? I do. About the boys, Alfred and Albert I can manage very well but don't you think it would be unwise to display their mother's ignorance as she could never learn those tumble-down affairs, I shall want a fresh supply of breath for every letter. And I know you will take the advice of an old friend. Mr Bodge says it is very unbecoming on the part of a father to name his sons after any king without ascertaining the extent of the child's brains. His sister Elizabeth thinks with him, as they have found in so many instances the name, instead of helping the child on in life, is a great hindrance; of course if they turn after their mother, there will be no frivelling on their part, but I must not fill my letter with descriptions of these unknown creatures. I must tell him how she is longing for the 27th. I have taken two comfortable little rooms for Mrs Thorndike and Isabella, 25/- for the week, they are very cosy; I think quite enough to give, don't you? As they will be with us a great deal, don't you think he had better drive from the station to the lodgings, leave their luggage and come up to us for high tea? This is what we propose doing. Willie came home from Oxford last night so we shall be a jolly party. Take care of yourself at Gloster, tell me your address; how shall you manage to get down on the Monday? I do hope, darling, you will take care of yourself for her sake. She feels exactly as he does. Life would be simply miserable without him now. I am so busy, dear, working. I want to work a banner screen for the study, with St John's Crest. Write and tell me if you have one, I don't remember seeing one in your room. Willie is going to give us a carved oak chair for the study. I have several things promised me. Now, sweet old Arthur, I must reserve more news for the next letter; don't you think I am a good girl with my letters. Fondest love and she does thank him so for his kind comforting letters and remains always,

His Own True
AGNES

Glen Luie, 18 June 1881

My Own Arthur,

I don't want Monday to come, and no letter for you, so I am writing a few lines tonight, as tomorrow (Sunday) is such a long day with me. I received your letter today about the servant. I must wait a day or two as I have asked Jane, a cook we used to have, to come to me; she would help do anything and I am so fond of her. She is living now with the rector of Haslemere and only left us because the stairs were so trying; we lived in a much higher house than we do now. She is such a thorough servant and so refined; perhaps she will not leave her present situation as she is very happy there, but Mother says she should never feel anxious if she knew I had Jane; when I don't happen to feel very well she would be such a treasure. I will let you know later. Now, darling, I was to ask his advice about another subject. She must tell him everything. You know Mr Copp who gave me that ring. Well! his ship is at Southampton; a few days ago he came up and I hadn't the heart to tell him of my engagement; he is so fond of me and I know he didn't know anything about it. He made me an offer two years ago, but you know I could not love him; nobody will ever be anything to her now but her own Arthur, she does love him so dearly. Now dear, am I, or ought I, to write him a note and tell him about it; it seems rather a shame for him to come to the house with the idea of gaining my love, he is such a good fellow at heart that I wouldn't hurt his feelings for the world. When he went away the other night he said, 'Be

51

sure and take care of yourself until I see you again,' and I never answered. Oh! Arthur darling, my protector and adviser, do tell your Agnes what to do; she does love her Arthur so dearly that she finds it hard even to talk to another man.

> Goodnight, you have all the love and sincere trust of your very own
> AGNES

My Very Dearest One,

He is so sorry she was disappointed thro' his negligence in not writing but, dear one, he was so busy that he really could not; he does hope that this letter when it did arrive dispersed her gloom, tho' he ought not to be so conceited as to think it could. Dear one, she must not think he minds her telling him anything and everything, it makes me feel you put such confidence in me and he pays back such a sweet trust so poorly; but dear, try and believe that he loves her more dearly for her confidence and he will try and be more worthy of it. *Do*, dear, tell him everything, and he would not like to feel that she was keeping back anything from him. Will she confide to him everything? He will be so happy if he may still feel confident in her. You ask me to forgive you, dear, for saying all you have; he does not like to deny her anything she asks but this is an impossibility. He cannot pardon what he dearly loves. He cannot forgive her for telling him all her heart, for it is his greatest happiness to know and feel that she does.

Dear, I wonder what she thinks of the 'general servant'. Has she written to her? I think it is quite worthwhile: I will write if you don't. I cannot help feeling it would be absurd to pay £15 to a servant. We should always be in trouble with her, and she will probably want a rise in her wages. If your mother is so kind as to give us £5 towards a servant it will be a great help and I believe we could get a good general servant for £7 or £8.

He must now get to his studies. Two sermons tomorrow. He will think of her all day.

With his fondest love.
He is her,
ARTHUR

Colston Parade, 20 June 1881

My Very Dearest One,

He does love her so for confiding to him everything. He does not the least mistrust her with Mr Copp. He sees, dear, that she is in somewhat of an awkward position – he cannot blame Mr Copp for liking her but feels so thankful that she is all his own – if I did not feel confident in this I should burn with jealousy; he thoroughly believes that she will not give him any cause for being jealous, dear one. On thinking it over, sweet one, he has come to the conclusion that she ought certainly to write to Mr Copp and tell him about our engagement, for he will be sure to know of it soon and it would be better for you to write and tell him than that he should hear it from any other source. He also thinks she ought to send him back the ring – it would not be right to keep it. I have therefore sent it to her – it has been a great effort to him to take it off, as she had put it on and consecrated it with a kiss and I could not have done it but from a sense that it was the right thing to do and I think she will be of the same mind. So will she send it to him. Though, dear, he has parted with her ring he still wears her bangle and has cut the initials A.T. (Agnes Thorndike) on it, meaning that when we are married he will give her back the link which she gave him and the bangle will represent the tie by which we are forever bound.

He would very much like to have a banner screen with St John's Arms, worked by her. I have often wished to have one and nobody has offered to work one for him and now this wish also is to be fulfilled by his own darling Agnes. He thinks she is a very good girl indeed about her writing – she quite helps him not to be miserable. Mr Bodge thayth when you are engaged take particular notice whether the young lady writes every day. Don't thay muth about it, but make a note of it if the doeth. Then you may be thure the loveth you, if not, you mutht look out that the ith not after thome other man.

Oh dear, how she did amuse him with her letter about the 5 Miss Thorndikes. Mr Bodge would thay if you are going to have 9 children take care that they are all boys then they can earn their own livelihoods and can carry on the family name to many generations, whereas the girls always change their name when they marry. Dear, we shall have to fit up the drawing room at Barley as a dining room for it will be a tight fit to sit down 11 every day. Now about Monday, dear, only a week, hurray!!

It would be nice for her to have Jane if she can get her. Anyone who is attached to you would not be likely to leave at the least provocation. I rather dread servants with high wages, they come for what they can get and not for love to the family, but if Jane who knows you so well can be got, she seems to be just the girl for us.

The Vicar came in here a day or two ago and I asked him if he would come and take part in the wedding. I explained all about your Vicar and he said of course that would be only right but he did not think he would be able to come owing to the examination during Ember week. He would be busy preparing for it; then he added, 'But if you would stay in Redcliffe I would come.' The dear Vicar has always got some nice thing to say and I thought it very nice of him to express a wish for me to stay.

It is very kind of your father to give you a piano; we can choose one when we go to town after our marriage. He must now finish this long epistle. Sorry, dear, he could not write yesterday. With his fondest love and a kiss.

He remains her own trusting
ARTHUR

My Very Dear Arthur,

I was delighted with your letter this morning. I haven't had an answer from Jane yet. Would you rather I put her off; only a very cheap servant in the kitchen is really so rare, and sometimes more extravagant, as they haven't any idea of management. Tell me, dear old thing, what I am to do. I am not so sure that Mother would give the £5 so willingly if we had an inexpensive servant; it was only on condition that we had one who understood things that she offered the extra. Of course Bertha would see the girl in Winchester if you think we had better. Fancy, dear, no word about the furniture; don't give more than he said without letting me see the inventory, if they are very high in their offer. I would rather have new but of course it would be cheap for the £150. I didn't mean you to go to Winchester at all, so you must have misunderstood my letter; Bertha leaves Winchester on the 27th and is coming here for the week, she might just as well meet you at Bishopstoke and all come on together so you won't have to move out of your carriage. Bertha will come to the Southampton train. I shall be at the Dock station as before. Do you know your movements after you leave here? Perhaps Mrs Thorndike will want you all to herself as you are to be separated so soon, but, dear Arthur, if you see the slightest chance of my being able to come, do let me won't you? I don't know how I shall let you go – I feel sure I shall be wretched and cry like a big baby when you are gone, so do what you can, there's an old darling.

Yesterday I was almost dead I had such a hard day, at school twice and in the evening went to St Mary's with Bertha, Fred Wilde, Willie and Bella; I was so quiet they all thought there was something the matter with me, but I couldn't get my spirits up a bit and only wanted to be left to think all about him. He was in my thoughts the whole of the service. Oh! dear Arthur, I don't know what I should do without you to come to in all my little troubles. I have such a lot to tell you when we meet. I stayed for the Holy Communion yesterday, the others all went home but

I couldn't turn away, darling, I knew he would like me to think of him and I did feel so happy after for not coming out. I am just going into the town to do some shopping, so goodbye, darling.

Fondest love from Your very own dear One

My Beloved and Dearest One,

He has not had a moment to sit down quietly to write to her before this, it now being 8.30 and he fears she will be disappointed if she does not receive a letter tomorrow morning. About Jane, dear, it is somewhat difficult for me to decide without having seen her or knowing much about her. If you think she is likely to be a true and faithful servant and fond of you, these are points very much in favour of taking her. The high wages are, to my mind, rather against it but, dear love, put on your prudent considerate cap and judge as you think best. Jack, you see, only gave his general servant £6. This is a great difference to £15. We shall be able to talk it over when we meet. Only six days more and my joy will be full. Oh love, I do long to press you to my heart again. I have positively hard work to go about my duty now, it seems all so bare and lonely. Dear one, give him a little encouragement to stick to his duty now. The one comfort he has is that soon she will be all his own, always together. Oh what joy!

Dear love, he is in a fog about his movements during his holiday. Mother and Isabella stay a week in S'hampton then return home. I should like to go to Barley that week and take her. Well, dear, I might take on the lodgings for another few days and then she could stay at Bath with him and he could take her and introduce her to his friends. She might stay on after the conclusion of his holiday and could come over to Redcliffe. Will she help him out of his fog? I think it would be better for me only to take a fortnight's holiday and then the Vicar would not object to my leaving a week sooner in September, for my time is not really up here till the 11th, but I want to leave on the 5th and go to Barley for a day or two and *then* to S'hampton to be joined to an angel by the holy tie of Matrimony. Then we should have a few more days for our London visit. In this case she had better come to Bath the week after Mother stays at S'hampton – *which* does she think best?

He must conclude, dear love, or miss the post, so with his fondest love and anxious care that she has recovered her fatigue.

He remains her ever loving,

ARTHUR

P.S. He wonders what she thought when she received the ring – he does miss it so much but he thinks he is right.

Glen Luie, 21 June 1881

My Own Darling Arthur,

I cannot describe to you my misery when I opened the case and found the ring I had put on your finger; I felt as though you had nothing now of mine and was half afraid to open the letter. I couldn't eat any breakfast and indulged in a fit of sobbing for almost half an hour; it was such a comfort to me when away to think of your having that ring on your little finger and now you have nothing to remind you but the bangle. Of course, Arthur darling, I will do as you wish in everything; you know I love you as dearly as a woman ever loved and feel sure if I were tried that I could die for you, so never mistrust me. Mr Copp I never loved or gave the slightest encouragement to but I feel sure he brought me home that ring as a little sort of curiosity – he brought Teddy one at the same time. This was a long time ago, months before he proposed to me so I know he never gave it as any engagement ring. Don't you think he might say, if I sent it back, that he never intended it in that light, as I never led him on at all and feel very much hurt he thought I should like one as it had the signs of the zodiac on it; don't think, dear Arthur, that I prize the ring at all for I never cared for the man, not any more than I could for Dick Cripps, and there is not much love there. If it is your wish, the ring shall go back, of course; I shall be guided by you in everything, for I love you so devotedly. Will you answer this by return; I will keep the note until I hear from you. I wish you would wear the ring. I don't think for a moment he thought I liked him when he gave it to me and perhaps might have forgotten he gave it to me, so will you, dear, still have the ring and I will send the note to him. I cannot let you be, dear, without a ring, so I shall wait anxiously for an answer and if you still think it ought to go back I will get a plain gold ring for you and have our two names put inside. She does love him so or the ring being taken off wouldn't have upset her as it did. I felt for the time broken-hearted about it. Now, Arthur dear, I would rather you came with your mother and Isabella, I should not like to think they were travelling alone. And the first time coming to Southampton I wouldn't like your mother to come alone; I think a son cannot be too attentive to his mother and I love you all the more for it, so don't let her come without you, will you? Don't say a word to them but I shall set up some flowers on the table in their sitting room. You are to be with us but, of course, we shall nearly always be together; how soon the week will be over; try and let me be with you, won't you?

I have given the wedding order for the bride's and bridesmaids' dresses and my own best dresses. The dressmaker will take quite a couple of months to complete the order. Would you like Canon Venables to come if the Vicar cannot, I do wish he could come, would it be any good if I wrote myself to him? I think I ought to write to Mrs Norris, don't you? Be sure you send me your address next Sunday, I want you to get a letter from me on that morning. I am very busy, I have worked one bracket and am doing a little strip of crewell work to put on a bookcase in our room; presently I am going to make a gooseberry pudding for dinner, so I am well employed. Yesterday a Mr and Mrs

Butler from Alton Hall and General West's widow called to congratulate me; they both kissed me so heartily and said they must see you; they are so fond of me. We are to drive there on the Thursday. We must accept this invitation, as they are such dear things. Their town house is at Portswood so we shall not have to go to Alton. Another day I thought Isabella, you and myself would go to Stockbridge and spend the day with Bertha's married sister, she has the sweetest place. We couldn't go more than three for the carriage won't hold more than three and we have a long drive from the station. We are all to go to Winchester as large a party as we like the day we go to Stockbridge. Willie, Bella and Bertha will take your mother somewhere. We will talk it over and arrange it. Oh! I could go on talking to you for hours but I mustn't, so Goodbye Darling

from your own
AGNES

Colston Parade, 22 June 1881

Dear Loved One,

How can he express his sorrow deeply enough at having caused her so much misery and how can he heal the wound he has so unintentionally made on her dear loving heart. He thinks if he gives her a little scolding it will do her more good than anything so prepare yourself for a tremendous rowing. To begin with she must not put such vast importance on things which after all do not matter much. She tells him, dear, that the fact of getting the ring back nearly broke her heart; these words were like hot burning coals to him, but, sweet one, she knows that he loves her dearer than his own life; therefore the fact of his returning a ring, which had been presented to her by another man who would have given the world to have won her for his wife ought not to have such dire and woeful effects upon her. There, dear, he feels he has quite scolded her and hopes it will mend her sore heart as he intends. Now dear, about sending the ring back to

Mr C. Of course it is a delicate point for me to decide as I am not aware in what way it was presented to you; if he gave it to you with any idea of tieing you to himself or as a means of making you love him in a way to become his wife I should not hesitate in saying send it back; but if he only gave it to you as you say, dear, as a curiosity, just for common friendship's sake or if he would think that you wished to cut him off from being a friend by returning it this would rather alter the case and I see no reason why you should return it. Now, dear, he will make a confession to her. It would be very difficult for him to disconnect Mr Copp's name from the ring. Whenever he saw it, tho' her image always came before him, there was somehow a feeling of Mr Copp connected with it. Would she be angry, dear, if he said that he would so *infinitely* prefer her sweet suggestion of getting a plain gold ring with our names – Agnes and Arthur inside. Oh! how dearly he would prize it and there would be no connection with its memory of anyone but her own dear self and he would ever delight to gaze on it. Dear, he hopes she will not think that he did not like the zodiac ring: he liked it much because she had worn it and had given it to him but, dear love, he cannot help saying that he would much prefer having one she gave him herself. He will give her half towards it, dear, if she will let him.

He hopes, dear, this will soothe her troubled spirit and give her comfort. I would certainly write to Mr Copp.

> With his fondest love to his wounded Agnes,
> He still remains as firmly as ever her own
> ARTHUR

Glen Luie, 22 June 1881

My Own Sweet Arthur,

I hope my letter did not displease you in any way. I shall look out anxiously for your answer. I have the most dreadful pen and cannot find another anywhere so I know you will excuse this badly written letter. Poor Mr Copp has heard of my engagement; he went to James yesterday and asked if it were true and said he had brought me home a lovely canary in a jolly new cage and taught it to be so tame only for me; he feels awfully down and told James he didn't think he could come to the house again; but, Arthur darling, I don't think I am to blame do you? For I never flirted with him and made him think I liked him; I always told him from the first that I had no love to give him. I do feel thankful I am engaged to you for I feel so happy but of course feel sorry for him; how I long to see you again and tell you how I love you. Don't laugh at me will you, but I always put your letters under my pillow at night; I couldn't sleep at all if I hadn't them, then if I wake up in the night I just take them, give them one little kiss, put them back again and go to sleep; don't you think this child is very absurd?

Bertha is going to Winchester today. Willie and Fred Wilde are going to get a high dog-cart and drive her home; of course I have to play chaperone but feel half afraid of their driving, they are such careless creatures. Bertha is quite jilting poor Fred; she says she doesn't really care for him at all; he hasn't enough go in society for her, so the poor men are in rather a muddle, aren't they? I never know what it is to have any mistrust in you, Arthur, for I know you really love me for myself and I do (I'm afraid to say it) almost worship you, you *scrumptious* old pet, so there is not much fear of our not being happy. Will it be asking too much of you, dear, to put an old sermon in your portmanteau, and preach at Trinity this Sunday morning? I long to hear you again; then in the evening we will all go to St Mary's. My children at school are so downcast at the thought of my leaving them, they all threaten to leave the school as they couldn't bear to see anyone in my place, poor little mites. I must give them all a parting gift. Now, darling, I cannot write more as I am so busy. Fondest love and a great big kiss, much bigger than the one you sent me,

I am your own One,
AGNES

My Own Darling Arthur,

I think I quite deserve the *severe* scolding you have given me and I do hope you will forgive me for vexing and troubling you so. I was very stupid to take it so much to heart but I certainly did at the time. I felt sorry after my letter had gone as I know you wouldn't hurt my feelings for anything. He will forget all about the stupid ring. I shall get one for you and give it to you next week with our names inside.

Now, darling, about your suggestion. If Mrs Thorndike and Isabella go back to Bath at the end of the week and you think it would be wise to go to Barley, of course there is your bedroom here as long as you like, I wouldn't hear of your taking on the lodgings. I should like to return to Bath with you so much for a week or a little more; shouldn't I enjoy one more Sunday at Redcliffe before you leave and spend the day in your rooms? Isabella would come with me. I think this a most glorious plan; do keep to this arrangement, won't you, dear? I went to Winchester yesterday to see Bertha home and slept the night, so have just returned. I cannot write a long letter as I shall only just catch the post and I know you like to hear from your Agnes. She feels quite happy now she has had his letter and quite thinks the scolding has had the desired effect; hoping she will never be so silly again and with every morsel of her love,

> She is and always will be his own penitent and true,
> AGNES

My Own Agnes,

She cannot think what comfort her letter brought this morning. For some reason it did not arrive till 12.15 and all the morning he was wondering whether his letter had so pained her that she could not write to him and then, when her loving dear letter came, it was too delightful. He was quite glad at the suspense of her letter that he might enjoy the receiving it as he did. She will have received his letter about the ring by this time and he does hope it will not add to her pain. Dear one, he will have the zodiac ring back again if she really wishes it and that will save putting her to the expense of buying another. I wish Mr Copp could have heard of your engagement first from you, dear, but I don't suppose it would have made much difference in his feelings. Of course, dear love, she could not help Mr C falling in love with her, but I am so thankful that she has reserved her love for me. And now I have got it I mean to keep it, for it is much too precious to part with. Her sweet face is always looking at him in the photo which is placed in *her* frame on his table. She said, dear, he had nothing of hers, but the bangle. She has forgotten the knife, the frame, gloves and book; quite a forgetful Donnie. Dear *One*, she quite feels she has got him under her pillow (not thumb) every night packed away in an envelope – she thinks to suppress him in that way does she, and bring him out when she wants a little comfort and at other times to squash him down by a pillow; he is quite ridiculing his Donnie. He hopes she got back safe after her drive, he feels quite anxious about it. I pity Fred Wilde if Bertha throws him over; how fickle is woman except his little woman; don't tell Bertha I said so, she might not like it, but I can't help thinking it a great shame if a woman leads a man to suppose she loves him then throws him over.

Dear love, how can he ever repay such true genuine love as hers is? 'She loves him better than ever any woman loved. She is sure if she were tried she could die for him.' Can I ever forget such love as this? *Never!!* But sweet one, she must not go too far. She must not worship him; that alone must be given to another far higher and better than he is. Dear, he quite sees what she means, but he feels that there is a danger in loving an earthly object too much and he fears that it may detract from the love and worship we owe to our Father. Let us, dear love, be careful not to allow our true and sincere love and devotion to each other take away from the love we owe Him. She must put me in the second place, dear, not in the first. He has quite preached her a sermon. How tired she will soon get of him if he is always preaching at her. Mr Bodge says if you marry a clergyman don't allow him to preach at you; he will want to exercise his preaching powers on his wife but Mr Bodge says, and Elizabeth coincides with him, like the two triangles in Euclid's 4th proposition – 1st book. Don't you put up with it but tell him plainly, 'Thtop your preaththing.'

He must now, dear, go to tea alone and then get ready for his discourse tonight.

With his fondest love and two kisses to make up for her big one, He remains now and ever *Hers*.

Colston Parade, 23 June 1881

My Own Loved One,

He must drop her a line before the post goes in $\frac{1}{4}$ of an hour. He has just had his communicants class for young men. There were 12 there, 3 being young women who had no business there, tho' they want instructions as much as the rest. My subject was repentance and a steadfast purpose of amendment. He hopes she has recovered from the misery he threw her into, dear sweet one, and he hopes she will understand his feelings about connecting the ring with Mr C without even wishing to. Dear, will she give him a ring, not one given by any man. He does hope she is not offended with him for this wish.

He has decided, dear, to come back to Bristol on Monday and then leave at 2 to pick up Mother and come thro' Salisbury, arriving at Southampton at 7.52. She must be there to meet him or he will be very disappointed. Will she decide on what day to go to Barley. Mrs Gordon wrote to me to ask you to let her know what day next week. I enclose her letter. Dear one, she must not mind this short and hurried letter as time is short for posting. So with his fondest love,

He remains,
Her loving and adoring,
ARTHUR

Colston Parade, 24 June 1881

My Dear One,

He has only time to scribble just a line to her tonight. He has been so busy getting the School Treat subscriptions in this afternoon which now amounts to £24.6 and he wants to get another £10 in hand before he leaves tomorrow. This being St John Baptist's Day we have a service at 7.30. I expect to hear the ringers strike up every minute but I must pay a 2d fine in order to send my Agnes a line, for after service we ring again and then I am going to Mrs Norton who is working some crewels for me (as I should say). So, dear, she must not mind getting such a scribbly letter this time; he will try and make up for it. He has got a piece of news for her to treasure up in her dear mind, something that happened to him today. He went into the town and got a lot of his hair cut off, now what does she think of that?! He feels he is very absurd but only following her example. She told him she was, so he must be. Has she decided what day to go to Barley? What do you say to spend Sunday there? Oh, no, that won't do for they have got a L[ocum] T[enens] now. Mrs G wishes us to go early in the week if we wish to find the house uninhabited.

With fondest love,
He is her,
ARTHUR

My Darling Arthur,

Your second letter yesterday was indeed a treat as it came so unexpectedly. About Barley, dear, don't you think it would be better for us to go there the beginning of the week after next, then I could return to Bath with you, as next week we have so many engagements. On Tuesday Mr Owen's meeting which he has made me promise to go to; Wednesday I forget what there is on, Thursday we dine at the Butlers, Friday we all go to Winchester for the day, see the Cathedral; in the afternoon all the young people will go to the tennis club and Mrs Thorndike and Mrs Thring can come with us if they feel inclined. On Saturday we will have some people here for tennis or go to Woodimer, so you must see our time will be taken up.

Now, Arthur dear, is it quite proper for me to go to Barley with you alone? I don't see any reason why we couldn't; if it is not, I can get Amy to come and she is such a capital little wife so that she could say in a minute what we should want and have a good look about the house, duckey. I am looking forward to Monday; it will be delightful. Bertha will be at Bishopstoke. Fancy seeing you so soon; I have quite recovered from my stupid miserable feelings and feel rather ashamed of myself for having given way to them. I feel sure you have forgiven me, so I am in good spirits. I am just off to play the organ for service. I hope I shall be able to come to Redcliffe Church one Sunday; I should feel happy if I might; I don't see why we cannot manage it. I had to choose the material yesterday for my wedding dress; you cannot tell what a strange feeling came over me, it seems such a dream; I cannot imagine this idle romping girl a married woman. Well, dear old pet! I chose the most lovely quality satin and gave directions about the making. It is to be 2 yards and a half long, most perfect train, tight fitting body and such a long veil and chaplet of orange blossom round my head. My travelling dress is chosen, myrtle green silk made short but a train to loop on for evening wear, brocaded stamped velvet jacket same colour and large velvet hat with feathers; I think, darling, you will like it awfully, only I must not think too much of my dress, must I? Now, Arthur dear, I must hurry off to church, so with love to her loved one, she remains,

Always his own,
AGNES

Glen Luie, 25 June 1881

My very Own Arthur,

Your letter yesterday was such a comfort to me. I think I read it through about forty times and devoured every word of it. I have a plain gold ring for you and will give it to you on Monday. We will forget all the little feelings about the other; poor Mr Copp. I do pity him very much; the canary has been sent to Amy, he was determined one of the family should have it. Now, darling, about our servant. I had a letter from Jane this morning; it is her great wish to live with Mr Strange and they have promised if their present cook doesn't suit, to take her, or she would have come to me in a minute, so it won't do to persuade her to come against the Stranges. I will write to Winchester about that girl and let Bertha see her on Monday before she comes down; perhaps we may get a good one for less. I will tell you a little of movements. Last night Mr and Mrs Hickenam took me a ticket for *H.M.S. Pinafore* at the theatre. I had seen it before in town but felt obliged to go after their taking the ticket. I did wish you had been there for I do think I looked rather nice; I had on my white silk with dark rose buds, but I didn't want to captivate any of the young men; and when the lovers were so awfully sweet on the stage she thought of him all the time and wished he had been sitting by the side of her. I am longing to see *Olivette* at the Strand, I know he will take her if she behaves herself like a good girl; fancy our being married and going about together, can you believe it? I can't! Shall you take me to see your cousins? What fun we shall have and how lovely it will be to think that nothing will be able to come between us. I should so like one Sunday at Redcliffe and just see the people once more. Promise me, if I am at Bath, to manage this for me, won't you, Arthur dear? I know you couldn't say (no) to such a touching appeal; won't she be able to get over him when she wants her own way? He is so *delicate* and she is so *showy* that she feels sure he will be so frightened when she speaks that he will immediately (obey) without the slightest hesitation! Now, darling, I have oceans of little things to do today so reserving all other news till we meet and with my very fondest love and three great big kisses. She is always his obedient,

(I mean loving)
AGNES

The Paragon, Bath, 25 June 1881

My Own One,

Just a line before going to see the lawyer about money matters. He will not be able to write from Cerney, he fears.

About Barley, dear, Mrs G wishes we would come early in the week. I should like Mother and Isabella to come to Barley so as you say you have made no arrangements for Wednesday why not write to Mrs Gordon and say we will go on Wednesday. Mrs Gordon will put you 3 up at the Rectory and I can go to the curatage so, dear one, had she not better write to Barley and say we will come Wednesday. My address tomorrow is c/o the Rev. Canon Medd – Rectory – North Cerney – Cirencester.

Good-bye, dear love. Only two more days. Did like her letter so much. They always give him such comfort.

With his fondest love, he remains,
Her own One

Dearest One,

He cannot go to bed without writing a line to her to tell her of all the events which happened after he lost sight of her beaming face at Salisbury. She may have noticed a person (male) sitting opposite him when he seated himself in the 3rd class carriage. Well, strange to say, at a station, the name of which I am not acquainted with, he recognised a friend on the platform; he rose in great haste and having thrust his head and a great portion of his body out of the window (luckily the door was well fastened or he might have had a nasty accident) well, having thus advanced his stately body nearer his friend, he called out 'Halloa' where-upon his friend gave him a hearty shake and introduced his sister who is going out next week to America – How touching! What do you think for? I expect you have guessed already – to be married! She looked very happy but I wondered how she would feel when she got on board and was tossing about on the briny ocean. Cobbleton is not a very pretty name is it? Fancy anybody marrying such a name. When I arrived at Westbury, the guard we spoke to at Salisbury addressed me with some common remarks and I entered into conversation with him, which so flattered him that he ushered me into a first class carriage and said he would make it all right. What a delicate attention, was it not? And there was poor Agnes travelling 2nd class. He wishes he could have given her his comfortable carriage. He hopes she had no trouble about her luggage and ticket and has arrived safely. His room looked so cheerful when he arrived. Mrs C had put up white curtains and filled the grate with white satin sort of material.

> Goodnight, dear One, and God bless her,
> He remains her loving,
> ARTHUR

My Arthur,

I haven't, as you may suppose, very much news, but I cannot let the day pass without writing; you cannot tell, darling, how I do miss you, it seems such a blank without you. I don't think I could exist more than six or seven weeks; how people manage to wait five years, I don't know, although if I were tried, I know I should wait 1000 years for you; I must tell you once again, Arthur, that I love and trust you with all my heart. It will be so lovely when we are always together and able to help and guide each other. I am quite longing for my useful life; I seem to have been so lazy lately. We have just come from the Park; we saw that afflicted man in the bath chair and his wife talking to him and I couldn't help thinking if you were in his place, how my happiest hours would be walking beside you and trying to cheer you, but I pray, darling, we may never have such a trial. Oh! how I long for Thursday! I do think and pray for him so and only hope some day to be worthy of him.

His Own Fond,
AGNES

Colston Parade, 19 July 1881

My Dearest One,

He must just write her a line before the post goes out tonight to tell her how much he misses the sweet smile and kiss he has been enjoying for the last three weeks. How he would like to have one now. He has had another present, dear: one we both so much wished for. It came very unexpectedly and for some time I was in ignorance who it came from. At last I found a paper with 'from Canon Venables' on it. If I were to leave you to guess till next week I don't think you would, so I suppose I had better tell you. A 'guest' table like the one I gave to Mother. Would you like to take it home with you? If so I will pack it up again.

There was a Band of Hope Meeting tonight and we had plenty of singing. I sang 'Barbara Allen', accompanied by Mrs Francombe because there was no Agnes at hand. The Italian is becoming quite a nuisance. He thinks it necessary to come and sit in my room of an evening; he is very good, natural sort of fellow but rather tiresome to talk to as one has to repeat the same thing over so often. Tomorrow night I have my communicant's meeting which I must now prepare for: preach on Thursday, Friday, Sunday afternoon. Hopes he will get a letter from her tomorrow morning.

> With fondest love and a kiss,
> He remains forever her own adoring,
> ARTHUR

Glen Luie, 24 July 1881

My Very Own Arthur,

I tried very hard to find time to write last night but could not possibly manage it, so do forgive me, darling, for not doing so. I arrived home quite safely and tried to fancy him eating his pork pie at Salisbury. I did feel down in the mouth after leaving him; it is such a trial for me, but I hope to keep up my spirits; after all the joyful part, I think it would be ungrateful to murmur; how lovely the meeting will be. I have just come home from Sunday School. I went to the Vicarage and had some ginger-beer I was so thirsty, the vicar was so sweet and talked to me so beautifully, just as *he* will talk when we are one. Darling, I shall come to you in all my little troubles and I know he will help me if he can; she will try with all her might to be a good girl, though she cannot do much in her own strength, but must be guided by One much holier and better than she is. Arthur, dear, will you see if September 16th can be arranged for the wedding, as the beginning of next month the invitations will be sent out. I feel that my love increases more and more every day. She will worry him with all her affection but, dear, I quite remember to do the right thing in the right place and as my future husband with his (QUIET COMMAND) would wisely say, 'I shall be very grieved if there is anything left undone in the afternoon which ought to have been done in the morning.' Well, sweet thing, she quite understands all this and any suggestion he can make for her good will be welcomed by her.

I saw Alice Wallis this morning, she was most agreeable and quite fell in with me in everything. She wants a little quiet talking to, then she is all right. Bella sends her love to you, she was so pleased to get me home. I do hope you are not seedy now; if you are, do take care of yourself for my sake and ask Mrs Carter to nurse you, only you mustn't let her stroke your dear, old, thin back, for that is my special property and I cannot allow anyone but myself to feel his darling bones, isn't she rude? Nevertheless, darling, she loves him and he wouldn't like to have a half-and-half sort of love; she gives herself and all her love to him and she hopes he will always love and cherish (as she does him) His Own Devoted,

AGNES

P.S. Will write tomorrow.

Colston Parade, 10.40 pm, 25 July 1881

My Dearest One,

Just a line before going to bed that you may not be disappointed on Monday. He has thought about her all day and it has given him much pleasure doing so. I was much disappointed that so few of my class came to Holy Communion and I had to give them a good dressing for it in class. The Vicar preached in the morning on the Epistle – 'The animative, earnest, heart stirring language of St Paul.' I preached in the afternoon on 'choosing for eternity.' One point I brought out was – Always when about to make a choice in anything, offer up a silent prayer, and, dear,

I am so thankful I was helped to do this in making my choice for a wife, and it is for this reason I have not the very minutest regret in the choice I have been led to make. Dickerson gave us a very powerful sermon (in 2 senses) both in matter and power of voice, the subject being David's sin with Uriah and Bathsheba, especially bringing out the deceitfulness of presumptuous sin, how it blinds the eyes and corrupts pure motives.

I took tea with Mr Hatherly today and he showed me a wonderful lot of letters he had from every Bishop and Archbishop, Lords and other swells, when he was collecting for the cathedral at Newfoundland. He got over £13,000. It was very odd, I met Mr H at Salisbury returning to Bristol and he made the journey home so pleasant that I was thankful to have met him. I hope, dear love, she had a pleasant journey after the sweet (I can't help calling it sweet) farewell we had. I shall think of the smile she gave him as the train moved off till we meet again. I feel quite ashamed at not having answered Bella's letter. Do tell her that it is really from stress of duty that has prevented me doing so. I hope to be able to do so tomorrow. I hope you found them all well at home. How delighted they must all be to have the life of the house back again. I have heaps more to tell you but must reserve it as 'tempus fugit'. So, dear One, with all his fondest love and kisses, He is her own,

ARTHUR

Glen Luie, 25 July 1881

My Own Darling Arthur,

I must write you a letter today, although I don't seem to have much news. I am going into the town this morning with Alice Wallis to do some shopping. You cannot tell how miserable I felt last night in Church. I did pipe just a little, for we had a most affecting sermon from the Vicar about David and Absalom; his text was 'Deal gently with the young man'. I never heard a better sermon and I did wish *he* had been with me, but it cannot

73

be; how shall I endure the next few weeks? When I think of him having all his meals alone it seems too dreadful, so mind you have plenty to do so I shall be kept out of mischief. I hope Mr Gordon will soon write about the furniture, it will be quite a weight off my mind to get it settled. I do so long for September; how lovely it will be to have you with me always. The Vicar told me yesterday to be sure and give in as much as possible to my husband and not have any secrets from him, then he knew we should be happy. Now, my old pet, I must say goodbye for another day, so with fondest love and kisses,

She is, for ever, your own
AGNES

Colston Parade, 26 July 1881

My Own Dearest One,

I have been so busy all day in Church with services, marriages, ringers and certificates that I have really, dear, had not a moment to write to her. I have just returned from Mrs Norton's with whom I had supper after service and played bagatelle. She has given us one of those figured antimacassers and Miss Hill another and a third is coming, so we shall be well off for them at Barley. Mrs Hatherly sent me a large-sized print of St Mary's which I shall value very much. Shall I send it? Your friend would frame it cheaper than I could get it done here. Oh, dear love, I cannot tell you what inexpressible delight your sweet letter gave me this morning. I could not help thanking God for giving me such a true genuine and sincere one to love and to cherish; I do believe that as He has brought us together and bound us by such a strong tie, He will keep us that we may both live to His praise and honour and this will bring us the greatest and most enduring happiness.

Dear love, has she any very particular reason for fixing on a Friday for our marriage festivities? Would not the 15th be equally convenient? Unless she has some very particular reason for choosing Friday 16th I should prefer it not to be on that day of the week. I heard from Barley today but not a word about the furniture; I shall get another letter tomorrow about 'businesses'.

Mr G has been away. He likes his L.T. and he says he is very careful over the goods of the curateage. I must ask him to let me off Sunday 18th. I dare say it will not make any difference, as his L.T. may be able to stay any length of time. Mrs Norton, Miss Hill and Miss Standswich came in to see my screen which they had a hand in and they admired it very much. There is another day gone and I have not written to Bella what will she think of me. Do ask her, dear, to forgive me as I have been so busy today with Church and vicarage meetings. I hope to have more leisure tomorrow.

And now, dear heart, I must go to bed. I fear you will not get this by the usual post. I feel that 'absence but brightens the eyes that I miss, and longing but heightens the spell of thy kiss'.

Goodnight, sweet love, may angels guard and protect you in the earnest prayer of your ever fond and loving,

ARTHUR

P.S. Did I leave a coat in my room at your house?

Glen Luie, 26 July 1881

My Own Arthur,

I felt a little disappointed this morning at not getting a letter by the mid-day post but suppose you are awfully busy arranging for the school treat. Be sure you take care of yourself and not get over-heated again. It quite worried me your looking so seedy, so, like my own sweet thing, attend to these instructions, they come from a *wise woman*. Your letter last night was a great treat, how I do sit down in a quiet spot and devour every word. I am so glad, dear, to think you don't regret your choice of wife. I feel placed in a responsible position with such a dignified (*person*) to look after; I don't think either of us regret it and I do sincerely believe that you love me and as for my love for you, why,

75

duckey, you will never know the end of it. I have been very busy this morning; when I know about the furniture I can have the drawing room curtains made, but I must wait until the furniture is decided. Let me know as soon as you can. I do long for the time – what a lovely happy day it will be; fancy, Arthur, my being your own wife, it seems too splendid, our cosy winter evenings. Do, darling, I implore you take care of yourself for my sake and don't work too hard to please anybody. Won't I take care of you at Barley; you will be quite under my care, I shall not assert my authority all at once but I am full of quiet command. Now, sweet love, Goodbye for another day,

Fondest love and kisses,
From his own Dear One

Colston Parade, 27 July 1881

My Very Dearest Old Thing,

Having amused myself for half an hour with soft melody (I fear the time was not very accurate) on the piano I think the pleasure of writing to you will come like sunshine after a thunderstorm. I only hope it may have a similar effect upon you. I doubt if you will relish having letters from me if I treat you as I did the last, for I find my letter was not stamped for me as I expected. I enclose 2d for my stupidity in not providing myself with stamps before everybody had gone to bed and shops all shut. Anyhow I risked the result rather than risk the displeasure I might possibly have caused if I had failed to write at all. Don't be disappointed if you do not get a letter on Friday for I don't see how I can write after the School Treat. We shall not be home till about 10. Dear love, I am very happy, not, dear, because you are away, that would be too dreadful an idea to harbour for a moment, but because there is an inward joy at possessing such a valuable and true love. In the midst of my duties it comforts me and encourages me. I have often to exercise self-denial by putting the thoughts of his Agnes away; but it is hard work to do this. Oh, dear one, how I shall welcome the month of September – fancy only one month between July and September. If she tries to be happy and cheerful about her duties for his sake the time will pass much quicker than she anticipates. Only don't sit down and mope and long for the time to pass quickly for it will only make you feel discontented and as you say, dear, we ought to be so thankful that we have not had to wait a longer time. I think the vicar was wise in his advice about having no secrets from me. Nothing would harbour mistrust more in each other than this. So, dear, be perfectly open and straightforward in everything with me and I shall love you still more deeply.

Dear One, I have just received a long letter from Mr Gordon and he tells me Mr Barnes was very dissatisfied with the price of valuation and thought of employing another man but he was afraid of the trouble and expense so has decided to let me have it for 'what do you think?' And that provided I pay it at once, which Mr Gordon was afraid I should not be able to do, and again I must let the furniture remain for the use of Mr & Mrs Drive, who are very careful people, and if anything is broken they would replace it. Well, Mr Gordon thinks it a great bargain for if I had bought the same things new they would have cost three times as much, and the carriage down and fixings would come to about £20, he thinks, so I do not fancy I can do better than accept the offer and send him a cheque. By the bye I have not yet told you how much he wants for it; how you must be dying to know. Well, it is good sometimes to exercise a little patience, for you will have to put up with a great deal from me, I can assure you. So dear, what you had better do is to practice patience; I don't mean the piece of music I gave you, but the virtue. Mr G also says a great deal about servants; a former curate only had one female servant for a year. He seems bent on our taking James as Jack-of-all-works. Well, dear, now I will satisfy your curiosity for I feel if I do not, your patience will be quite exhausted and all belonging to her is too precious to be exhausted. Well, he keeps to the same sum that Mr G mentioned and the upholsterer – namely £180, provided I pay it at once (within a week or two).

How beautifully everything is turning out for us and how thankful we ought to be. Good night, sweet love. God bless and keep you,

Your own,
ARTHUR

Glen Luie, 28 July 1881

My Ever Darling One,

How can I ask your forgiveness for not writing yesterday; the truth is I had to go to Southsea by the 9 o'clock boat so could not possibly find time before then. When I arrived at Southsea, my cousins had not seen me since my return from Bristol so you can imagine the fuss. I asked for paper and pen but they hid everything away and declared that I shouldn't write a line but talk to them all the time. I did pass such a miserable night and couldn't get it out of my head. They made me miss the boat and, of course, I slept there but came home by train this morning. Not another day do I leave home; just tell me, darling, that I mustn't miss writing another day and scold me well if you like, for I quite deserve harsh treatment. I hope Bella explained my going off. Now Darling, about Mr Gordon's letter, you have done quite right about the furniture, settle it as quickly as you can before they can recall anything. I do call it a great bargain and am so delighted it is not more. About the general servant, we cannot put off Elizabeth now, she could not cook; I shall call the servant a general servant I engage so that, darling, if we had a child, Elizabeth with my help could manage. We couldn't keep them, dear, could we and in a country house with only two in family; it will be a very easy place if we have the gardener as first arranged at 10/- per week* and the rector gives the two. We could try it for a few months and see how our finances stand. I do think

* This does seem a great deal of money in the light of what they were spending on a general servant but her letter definitely says 10/- a week, though it could possibly have been a slip on her part and she really meant 10/- a month. We are never likely to know.

three days a week enough but let us give him a trial, and if we find we cannot manage it, must tell the rector so; these other people seem to have had more than we do. Darling, write and tell the vicar one young servant is engaged and we must get another to cook for us. So, to begin with, you will give the man 10/- as first arranged, if he gives the two extra. I will return Mr Gordon's letter tomorrow but do as I have said; after we get settled a little bit we can soon arrange matters. I do hope, darling, you will forgive me for not writing yesterday, it really wasn't my own fault but it has been praying on my mind all day. Sweet old Arthur, it isn't neglect on my part, for you know how dearly I love you. Hoping you weren't angry, as you had just cause to be, I am

Your Own Penitent,
One

Glen Luie, 28 July 1881

Dear Loved One,

Two letters today to make up for not writing yesterday. I quite forgot to answer your questions about the Friday, I thought the 16th came on a Thursday. I wouldn't think of being married on a Friday; you can arrange it for the Thursday or Tuesday, either the 15th or 13th and let me know, Darling. Would you mind sending me the book for the Stores.* I suppose you have a book, we don't belong to the same; I want to look through and make a list of some things we shall want. Mother asked what I should like Teddy to give us. I have chosen a dessert service to match exactly the plates at Barley so that we have now a full set; I thought if Bella gave us a pretty dinner service we must have these things. Oh! it is such a pleasure getting all the things, I shall take the greatest interest in my home and *husband*. If it isn't bothering you too much, dear, I would send the view of Redcliffe, as I can get it framed. When your goods go, mine shall

---

* Army & Navy Stores.

meet them. Now, sweet pet, goodnight. I do wish I could give you just one long kiss, but I am not allowed.

I am always your very own,
AGNES

[Here the sequence of Agnes's letters ends until September 9, just six days before their wedding.]

July 28th

Glen Lui
Loch Awe

Dear loved One,

Two letters today to make up for not writing yesterday. I quite forgot to answer your questions about the Friday. I thought the 16th came on a Thursday. I wouldn't think of being married on a Friday.

MS. of Agnes's letter dated 28 July 1881

8 Paragon
Bath
Monday 7.15.

My own dearest One

I have been so miserable about you all day at the thought of your being low-spirited & suffering. Mostly on my account. thro' my stupid nonsense. I shall look out so anxiously for a letter tomorrow. but perhaps she will not write. as she has

PS. Mother, Isabella & St. all send love. Brother is trying you have a toothache. pray pray you had better come here & you would soon get well, think so too. I think you had better take a little medicine. AJ.

MS. of Arthur's letter dated 30 July 1881

82

My Own Dearest One,

I have been so miserable about you all day at the thought of your being low spirited and suffering, and mostly on my account thro my stupid nonsense. I shall look out so anxiously for a letter tomorrow, but perhaps she will not write, as she has got an idea in her head that she has been writing too often but I shall be grieved if one does not come, for I am so anxious to know how you are. After parish arrangements we were let off so I thought I would run over here to see Mother and Isabella. The latter is quite laid up, confined to the house for more than a week. She is better but feels quite weakened. Sister Julia has just come in and it is rather difficult to write while they are chattering but I hope I shall not say anything to offend her, Dear One. It was an unfortunate circumstance my mentioning my opinion of the girl gardener. Dear, he will not do it again but will be very careful not to say anything to pain his dear love. Dear, there seems to be some doubt as to whether Alfred Evans will be able to come. He is engaged as tutor to the Marquis of Bath for 6 weeks and he has some feelings about asking leave for two days but he will see when he gets there. Oh dear, you would have laughed if you had heard what an old woman said about my sermon last night. Mrs Carter told me, 'What do you think someone said tonight about you, "Well that dear young man did give us a good sermon tonight".' Now dear, she must not mind a poor old woman calling him a dear young man – it amused me very much. Dear One, I am longing for the 15th. Will it ever come? Most likely

Frank will get a fortnight's leave before the wedding. He might come down with me to Barley on the Monday and come on to you, then he would see what a sweet little home we are to have. I am getting on slowly with the duet – it is uphill work without the treble part but I hope to be pretty perfect on it before I leave Redcliffe.

I have not received the bridesmaids' bangles yet and the shops are all shut today. Dear One, before he finishes he must ask her not to have any doubts that he does not really love her, for he does with all his heart and can never care twopence about any other girl. So cheer up, dear love, and I pray this letter will have moved your grief. Goodbye, Sweet, and God Bless you and keep you in health is the fond wish of your own true,

loving,

ARTHUR

Colston Parade, 30 July 1881

Oh Agnes Dear,

Your letters today have been sweet indeed – why should I be repaid so fully for a little disappointment. If I had felt ever so much disposed to scold you for any supposed neglect on your part my soul has melted under the genial warmth of your sweetness and I feel, dear one, that this will always be the way between us if troubles or disappointments come. Your sweet disposition and loving affectionate heart will soon disperse the clouds and all will be sunshine again.

About the day for the wedding, dear, I am more inclined to fix on the 13th – Tuesday, for on Sunday I shall preach my farewell sermon and I fancy it would be better to leave on the next day. Then again, if it is necessary to go to Barley first to see about things myself it would be better to put it off till Thursday – but I do not think it would be really necessary for me to go to Barley first – I could make my arrangements by letter so I think we will decide on Tuesday the 13th. Only 7 weeks next Tuesday. Dear

One, I have not said a word about my neglect in not letting you get a letter this morning but he went off with the children at 9.30 and did not return till 9.30. Then I went and had supper with Mrs Norton. I hope, dear, she was not very disappointed, for he could not possibly help it. He will tell her all about the treat in his next letter,

With very much love,
He is her own,
ARTHUR

Redcliffe, 31 July 1881

My Own Beloved One,

He had not been able to write by the 9.30 post tonight for directly after the 8 o'clock service he had to go to choir practice so she will have to excuse him for his inability; she must feel quite a neglected one and he begs her pardon dear.

Now, sweet one, he will tell her of the doings during the two school treats. On Wednesday about 650 infants assembled at the vicarage. It was quite a pretty sight – they began by singing songs: then followed tea which was quite a business. I did not carry on with anybody dear except Miss Nelson and I sat next to her at tea, but Miss Brinsdon and Mrs Beggs sat opposite, so I had to be on my best behaviour. Of course, dear, she is now feeling quite jealous of Miss N and wishes she could have changed places with her, though soon she will not wish to change places with anybody, at least I am conceited enough to believe so.

After tea Punch and Judy was exhibited, much to the delight of the children who could not remain seated as ordered but rose with as much dignity as they could, at the first appearance of Punch in persona. Then more cake was distributed and they dispersed.

Yesterday was a much longer affair. At 9.30 all the schools assembled and marched to the station, the drum and fife band playing. The station was a sight. Every square foot was occupied by living beings, the poor little ones were nearly crushed by the parents. I had to act policeman by keeping the people back from the children. At last the train came in and all the arrangements were upset by the parents rushing into any carriage they could instead of getting in their appointed places. When the train was full, and it consisted of 18 carriages, we moved off and a second train was filled with toys. Altogether 1000 children and 400 grownups. When we arrived at Weston they got out as you may suppose and formed a procession, had a bun each given to them as they went out and marched to the beach where they enjoyed themselves in various ways. I got hold of a dozen young fellows and had a good game of rounders. Then took a walk with them to the pier which did not appear tempting enough to pay 1/- to go on, so we walked thro' the woods and I amused them by telling them anecdotes. Then we lost ourselves and found ourselves on the edge of a precipice. We did not try to go down but walked round and after searching about discovered a way down and, by following our noses, we soon found ourselves back at the station where they were preparing for tea. A shower of rain came on and we all thought we were in for a wet evening but luckily it kept off till we returned. The tea finished, we went on the beach again and I had a walk with a very charming young girl named Miss Gardner—not the doctor's daughter. She formerly lived in Redcliffe. She made herself very agreeable and chatted away '19 to the dozen'. I feel certain I have roused that jealous feeling again in your dear breast and she is thinking that he ought not to walk and chat with any young girl, especially if she is fascinating, lest she should induce him to give up his Agnes for the new one; dear, she must not have any feelings of this kind for she knows how truly and devotedly he loves her, and will never give his love to anyone but her and his love seems to get deeper and deeper every day. Her letter today sent a thrill of joy thro' his whole body and I could not help thanking God for giving me such a sweet one to love and cherish.

We all returned safe by 9.30 and I went and had a good supper with Mrs Norton and played bagatelle after. Mrs N has given us another antimacassar.

Past 11—must go to bed. Goodnight, dear love,

God bless you in your love,
Your ever fond,
ARTHUR

Colston Parade, 1 August 1881

Beloved One of My Heart,

I cannot think how it was you did not get my letter before yesterday morning. What suspense you must have been in, dear love. Now, dear, the cloud has blown over and all is sweet and congenial sunshine again only the full brightness is yet in store for me on the 15th. The banns are to be put up here in Redcliffe next Sunday week, as we settled—that is, the 14th, 21st, 28th August. Then the last two Sundays of separation we can spend in peace in our own parish church without having our names publicly proclaimed. She says she will not go to hear hers published and I think she is quite sensible in not doing so. Darling, the bridesmaids' bangles came this morning and they are very pretty. Our names are engraved on each. There are 4 different patterns on the bangles – of course all are the same shape. Isabella's is smaller than the rest, as she wished. Fancy, Dear One, only 6 weeks today. Oh, I am quite off my head with joy. At present I feel I can 'jump over the moon', as they say, with delight and excitement at the thought of only 6 weeks and I shall be with you – by this time we shall be in London as *Man and Wife*. Hoopla!!! I do feel in such a funny mood dear. It is your letter this morning that has done it and yet I ought not to be so happy when I know she is suffering with a sore throat. Do, darling, take care of yourself.

I saw a most lovely pier glass today, black and gold with a shelf each side and flowers painted in blue on a gold background in the two top corners – price £5.10 – ready money £5.5. Wouldn't your friend who offered the clock give us this? I could send it down to Barley with my things and have a picture of it to exhibit among the presents.

I do hope, dear, you will not be homesick. I will try very hard to make you so happy that you will not want to go home – at least to your mother's home. Your home will be Barley. I shall never forget that beautiful verse you sent me, dear love. I shall so delight in hearing every little thing either joy or grief she may have in her life and I do pray that God will guide me to do what is right in His sight – then, dear, I do not fear being able to make you happy, for your aim is the same and when two people strive together for the same purpose it is almost sure to prosper. I trust your mother's back is getting stronger – I don't think I half thanked her for her kindness to me while I was with you at Glen Luie but I can safely say I never enjoyed 10 days so much before as I did then. What does your father think of the bargain with the furniture? Give my love to all who care to have it and, darling, with much for her dear self,

He is now and always her very own,
ARTHUR

Colston Parade, 2 August 1881

My Own Beloved Agnes,

It was with the greatest delight I saw your welcome handwriting a few moments ago but my joy was soon turned to deep sorrow when I perceived that by my thoughtless joking I had really pained you. Oh, dear love, what can I do to heal the wound I have quite unintentionally made? She must know, dear one, that she is all the world to him, for he loves her better than himself – he would go through anything for her. He thought, dear, she would take no account of the little girl he spoke to for a few moments. I am sure I could not have talked to her, with some other teachers, more than $\frac{1}{4}$ of an hour and I never saw her before. So, dear, if I had thought for a moment it would have pained her, he would never have said a word about it but such an idea never entered his head. Agnes, dear, I have not been careful enough in what I have said. I do hope I have not many times before given her pain by my frivolous joking. Believe me, sweet, it gives me more pain than she can imagine to think I have caused her a single tear when she wants so much comforting under the trial of separation. I am so glad you gave me a good scolding – only I deserved a much worse one. Darling, if you were to give up writing every day I don't know what I should do. Your letters give me comfort and peace for the whole day and are always full of the deepest interest. Do not think, sweet love, I do not care for them, for they are the very joy of my life now I am away from you. I count the days and think 'well there is one day nearer the 15th'. I am glad you have fixed on the 15th for, on second thoughts, it would be better than on 13th both for you, dear, and for me. I should be able to send off my things to Barley on the Monday and if necessary could run down myself. The thought of the day makes my heart beat fast with joy. Oh, that I could now press you to my heart and hear that dear, tender heart of yours by assuring you how much I love you. Darling, I implore you do not doubt me. I have given you my heart and no one can be anything to me but you. What a thoughtless idiot I must be not to have known that such a letter would pain you. Dear, it does not give me any pleasure to rouse your jealous feelings but I fear my stupid letter must have conveyed such an idea. Do burn it, dear, and forget that I wrote it. If you do not, write and say you have forgotten all about it and forgiven me. I declare I shall run down to you to crave forgiveness but that would involve me in great difficulties, for the Vicar will be away this week and only Dickerson and self here. So do, dear, write and tell me you have forgiven me and that you have cheered up. Dear, she must go and see her doctor about her throat. She never told him of it before, how long has she had it so swollen? I fear, dear, you have been over-exciting and working yourself. Don't sing while your throat is sore or you will irritate the glands. Do take care of yourself for my sake and mind you see the doctor for your throat. Dear one, she must not go and sit by herself in her room and think, for I am sure it only makes you low-spirited. I must now rush off to the clerical meeting. I have not eaten hardly any dinner for grief to think I should have been such a fool as to say anything to grieve you. Oh, Darling, that verse you found was too beautiful and I do hope, dear, that this letter will heal your wound and cheer you up. I was only this morning putting all letters in order. I cut out the leaves from a lock up diary and put your letters in the cover so they are safe under lock and key and I shall often take them up and read for comfort.

> Goodbye, dear love – Do forgive me,
> for I am still your loving and true,
> ARTHUR

Colston Parade, 3 August 1881

My Own Dearest One,

How I devoured your sweet letter this morning. It has made me feel quite happy again. I do hope, darling one, I shall never again say and do anything to hurt you – I never will knowingly and if he does without meaning it she will extend her love over him to cover the multitude of his offence. Dear One, how different the same things appear under different circumstances. Your letter which I said seemed to lack that warmth of love and affection, on reading it again today, I do not think so at all. I can see dear true love and affection in every sentence, so I must ask you to forgive me again for having told a story. I was so glad to hear that there was a locket really ordered for me. How I long to have it. Dear, do send it directly it is finished and the likeness in it. Another day and no letter from Mr Barnes or Gordon. I hope he is not relenting after all, but I should think he would rather have £100 ready money than have to wait a longer time, for I shall certainly make him wait if he puts any higher price on the furniture. Old Gordon is a slow coach in writing – perhaps he took 2 or 3 days to send on the letters to Mr Barnes. I must finish this to let it go by the 1.25.

Dinner is on the table,

Her Own,
ARTHUR

Colston Parade, 5 August 1881

My Darling One,

I feel so happy tonight, have just come out from the service, had a fair congregation. I preached on the young ruler who came to Christ asking, 'What good thing shall I do to inherit Eternal Life'. Dear One, the subject gave me great comfort. Of late I have been thinking a good deal about money and whether I should have enough to make you happy and it has somewhat worried me but in studying for my sermon it seemed to come home to me not to think too much about riches for it only means sorrow – so, darling, we will try by God's help to trust in Him for our daily sustenance and as He feedeth the sparrows so will He feed us with temporal and spiritual food.

I have written to S.J. to ask her to give us a glass. I can get one here for £3.3 – black and gold with a shelf each side. I will write and ask Francis if he will accept your kind invitation to S'hampton. What a delightful party we shall be on that day. I don't think I shall ever forget it. Less than 6 weeks now, dear – I hope the excitement trouble of the wedding is not hurting your mother's back. Give my love to her and to the others,

He is more than ever,
Her own,
ARTHUR

My Own Dearest One,

She must not regret any more about anything she has said, though at the time my stupidity caused her so much sorrow. I am now so perfectly happy in your love that the unpleasant is swallowed up in the pleasant. We will put the blame on the foster brother. The banns are to be put up on Sunday week. Jack will be back so I shall not have the ordeal to go thro' of publishing my own.

Darling, I had a letter from Mr Barnes this morning, he seems to have been a long time getting my letter for he said, 'In answer to your letter *just* received'. I suppose it has been following him about. It is a v. nice letter and he expressed himself '*very* sorry at parting with his household goods and I have lost considerably doing so'. I am going to send him the cheque as soon as my banker has drawn the money out of the stocks which will not be until Monday. I will ask another man, a young curate Dancy – Jack knows him, to come to be groomsman, but I have my doubt whether he will be able to come as he is not very well off. If you will ask the other that will make up 7. Must go to the bank.

> Goodbye, dear love – Your ever loving,
> ARTHUR

Colston Parade, 8 August 1881

My Very Dearest One,

We have had such a day of it today. The Redcliffe Cricket Club took a coach and four and drove to Almondsbury, about 7 miles from Bristol, to play against the cricket club there. It was a very pretty place adjoining Mr Sykes's brewery in Redcliffe Street house and grounds. The drive was the best part of it as it was such a lovely day, but we got rather the worst of it in the field. We did not get back till 9.30. I could not help thinking how different it was to the day at Frenchay. It was hard work to keep up any real life in the game having none of the fair sex to cheer us on like I had at Frenchay.

It is so odd with Vic lately; whenever she sees a lady dressed in white with a large hat she runs to her and jumps about quite pleased; evidently she is thinking of you, dear one, and takes those resembling your dress to yourself.

Darling, she must not be angry at this short letter; he does so delight in getting her sweet ones. He does not deserve them as his are so uninteresting. Fancy, dear, this day week our banns will be ready for publication. This, dear, will go by the 4 am post. I hope, dear, she will spend a happy Sunday. He will think of her in the H.C.

With his fondest love,
He is her own, fond,
ARTHUR

Colston Parade, 8 August 1881

My Own Dearest One,

I must write before I go to bed, though I am very tired, it has been a hard day as usual; there being no teachers in the school it gives extra work, but still I have had a very happy day and you, dear one, have been continually in my thoughts especially in the Holy Communion. He thought of her and prayed for her and himself that we might both grow together in the Grace of God.

Mr Dickerson gave us a beautiful sermon tonight on the life of Solomon and his request for a 'wise and understanding heart' but, dear, while he brought out this wonderful request in deep feeling and language, he also drew a picture of Solomon after his fall, and it makes me troubled to think that a man like Solomon, who having tasted the wonderful goodness of God, could fall away, having a wise and understanding heart and yet to fail and the reason of such a fall was that the pleasures of the world allured his heart from the love of God. He broke the law by loving *many* and *strange* women who turned his heart away from God. I thought, dear, 'now I wonder if I, when I have enjoyed the happiness of a married life – I shall fall away from God,' the answer was not long in coming. It was 'no, my wife will be the one to help me on my difficult road to Heaven, not like Solomon's who led him away.' Then I thought this was selfish and I asked God to strengthen both of us, to help each other, that we might have the one motive firmly fixed before us, of doing only those things which will be for the honour and glory of God. The sermon gave me great comfort and I hope the fruits of it will grow and ripen on the barren soil of the heart. He feels, dear one, he has now been writing a sermon to her but it is so sweet to have someone to write one's thoughts to; here again is another selfish motive. Oh, *when* shall I ever be free from selfishness? It is very hard to do so living by one's self. I shall have good exercise for self-discipline when I possess such a sweet little woman for my wife. Now Darling, I must finish. Did like her letter so much this morning. Tell me, Dear, when you get this. With fondest love to herself and best remembrance to the others, and Father and Mother.

I am your very own confiding,
ARTHUR

Colston Parade, 9 August 1881

My Very Dearest One,

I have today sent off £180 to Mr Barnes in Whitby for the furniture; there was some delay in getting the money from the Bank of England and a power of attorney, so that is done and I feel very thankful that I had saved the money to be able to use it when it was wanted. Thoughts of that £50 often come up before me, and I think what a lot I might have done with it if I had it now, but, dear, I do not regret having given it to such a noble cause and I often fancy, well if I had not given it, perhaps I should not have got the furniture under £230 and so I should have been in the same position, minus the pleasure of having given to the church. The post this morning brought me some very pleasing letters, the first and most pleasing, dear one, was from, perhaps she will not like it if I tell her. Of course, dear, she will think he is going to say hers. Well she will not be far wrong if she does, for hers was the first he opened and devoured and it will be the best of them all, and he does not in the least mind saying that he loved it. The others, dear, were from various people. One from Frank who is at Killarney enjoying himself but he tells me he is ordered to take command of a flying column for ten or twelve days so that his Killarney fun is cut short; he was staying with some very nice people and two misses on the scene. He goes in for numbers because he thinks there is then safety but I think one good sound trusty string to one's bow is better than two or three doubtful ones. I have the one which will never break but will be true to the end and thro' eternity. I didn't half thank you for the trouble and expense you had in sending my coat. I now feel I am in your debt to the great amount of 1/-. Put it down to the account, dear one. Another letter was from Dandy expressing his regret at not being able to come and act as my groomsman. He has very good reasons. I wish I could hear from Alfred Evans. Have you sent out the invitations? So she must try and get one, and if A.E. cannot come – two men. I asked Edward Norris to come but he will be up in Wales and cannot manage it and the same with Frank and Hugh.

I fancy the green sage curtains will look very handsome. I am glad you chose them in preference to the black and gold which would have made the room look so very mournful. The cream lace ones will make the room look very cheerful and bright. What a capital little manager she is, dear. How well we shall get on together at our home. Oh, don't I long to be there, especially now you have bought a quilt for I and her to lie down on. Eider is so soft and nice that we shall never suffer from cold feet. I am sorry to hear you have these in winter for I was looking forward to warm my cold feet by your warm ones.

The dead gold plush and ruby for the tables will be very

handsome, shows her excellent taste – wonderful. How grand our mantel piece will look with S.J.'s glass and Bertha's deep fringe. Don't you think it would be a good plan to put your harp in the centre of the room with a chair behind it and the screen round the whole; i.e. harp, chair and player – what a pretty effect it would have, with this advantage that anyone preferring to hear the music without seeing the performer could go round behind the screen and listen or not as they pleased, for no one would see them and therefore they would not give offence by appearing uninterested. Isabella says she will have the covers in time, if she cannot do them herself she will get them done. Dear One, I am getting on slowly with my playing. I am trying to learn accompaniments then I may be of some use to her, but I expect it will take me a long time before I shall be good enough for such a particular *person* as she is. I had a letter from Mr Langford, my late vicar, and he has ordered a set of serpentine marble salt cellars mounted in silver – just the very thing we wanted, I am very fond of serpentine and mounted in silver will be very handsome. Isabella's godmother sent me a cigar case, very kind of her and quite unexpected, don't you think I might write to her and say thank you for your present but isn't it a pity I don't smoke!! I dare say she will change it for me and give me something else. The rest of my news I must reserve for my next but I feel I could go on writing for another hour but I must stop now as I have to write to Mrs Wrongson – oh, I beg her pardon – Mrs Wrightson, to thank her for the cigar case.

> With love to all and much for her dear self,
> He is her own,
> ARTHUR

Colston Parade, 9 August 1881

My Own Dearest One,

I have just heard the very sad news of the death of Archdeacon Randall. He was here last Tuesday and I knelt beside him on

96

Tuesday night during prayers at the Vicarage and he seemed to be perfectly well. His death has cast quite a gloom over Redcliffe, for he was so much beloved by everybody.

I was so glad, dear one, to get your letter by the 12 o'clock post. I hope she has recovered her fatigue which she felt after her hard work yesterday. Dear One, fancy her going into residence at the vicarage, it does make the time appear nothing. He will write to her, dear, as she wishes, only she must inform him before Saturday what time she gets his letters. The one I wrote yesterday went by the 4 a.m. this morning. This one by the 5.20 p.m. I hope you will get this tomorrow morning's first post, for it will be a much more convenient post to catch than the 1.25. I wrote to the Bishop to inform him of my intention of leaving his diocese on the event of my marriage and I said that my letter did not require an answer, so his reply was all the nicer. How lovely the spoons must be, I quite want to see them. It is very kind of Mrs Green and also of Crissy, as you call her, giving us a toast rack. Darling, I have been calculating all the expenses, bills, travelling, move and everything this morning. I think I shall be able to pay every bill, so that on our wedding day I shall not owe a farthing and have a £ or so in my pocket. Then I shall have my stipend clear which must last us till Christmas. Do you think you can manage on £50 for the first quarter? Then I should have £10 for our stay in town. You must get into the way of paying for everything at the end of the quarter with the past quarter's money. For instance, I shall get £35 as my stipend on September 29th – now that money must go to pay for the expenses till Christmas. I never like to get behind with my bills. Darling, she may be assured that he will write and let her get a letter in the morning when at the Vicarage. We shall be glad to have Jack here again, remember me to him and family.

> With fondest love,
> He remains her own,
> ARTHUR

My Very Dearest One,

I was delighted with your letter this morning, so full of hope and love. I am sure dear if she has such a pure motive to live a holy religious life, she will never be left to want. I always find such comfort in that text 'Seek ye first the Kingdom of God and his righteousness and all the necessaries of life and food and raiment will be added unto you'. Dear, I think she will make a very good little wife, for she loves him so dearly and a home where true affection fills all the rooms be it ever so humble, there is no place like home. Barley would be nothing to him without his sweet one to fill it with pretty walks, calling on new people and when we get known we shall be asked out to dinner probably. Sister Julia wrote to me this morning to say she would give us the glass if we both preferred it. She could not afford more than £3. 3. I can get a very pretty one here, black and gold with one shelf each side for £3. 3. or one with a picture of swans at the top for £5. 5 with two shelves. I thought I might add the two guineas and get the better of the two but I don't think I will because it would not then be Sister Julia's present. Write and tell me whether you would prefer this to the spoons and forks. Dear, Mother is going to make me a present of £25 when I am married. This will be a great help. I want to get thro' this quarter and pay everything on my last quarter's money and so not to touch what will come in September till after the wedding. Darling, her account of the reception she received at the Temperence Meeting was too delightful but it is only what she deserves, if they had driven you thro' the town and cheered you all up the Avenue it would only be a very small way of repaying you for your loving attention to the cause in that parish. I hope they will show how they ought to appreciate your worth in a more substantial way than a cheer (which I own is very delightful to receive) when you leave them for good. You may thank your vicar for me if you like for his kindness in appreciating and bringing out before his people the value of Agnes. I shall always feel grateful to him for his kindness to you, dear. I know, dear one, she did not tell me all about how they received her to praise herself but because he loves to hear all about her; so mind she always tells him everything. Certainly have your cards printed Mrs Arthur Thorndike. Dear, how well it looks,

> With fondest love to his sweet Agnes,
> He is her own,
> ARTHUR

Colston Parade, 11 August 1881

Dear Sweet One,

I was so glad to get your letter this morning but felt so sorry that you had been so disappointed at not getting my letter. I hope, dear, the one you got this morning fully explained to you how unable I was to do so, darling. I hope she won't think him neglectful, for he really could not help it as I was away from home from 9.30–6.40. There, dear, I feel that she has forgiven him because he has made a clean breast of it, but still he will be glad to have a letter from her to say so.

No wonder Mr Strange was amused at your tongs and heating machine. If ever I feel dull at Barley I shall ask you to perform on your tongs and machine, and I am certain I shall soon be dying with laughter. I shall be very curious to see this wonderful machine which is to help beautify my Agnes. I suppose you will lay in a store of tongs in case yours should get damaged. Jack would advise three. I had to pull my self together after and during the reading of the second lesson in order not to appear conscious of anything out of the usual course of things and I don't think I betrayed myself at all. Of course I thought the whole congregation would be looking at me so I became very interested in a chant book and had the place all ready for the Jubilate and I sang 'Oh be joyful' with such pathos. How I wish I could have been in the Vestry to give you a hug and a kiss which I am conceited enough to believe would have removed your shakings. I should just like to have seen anybody who would have *dared* to object to the marriage! I should not have been able to contain myself. His or her life would have been in danger if they had come within reach of me. But no one had the audacity to do this.

I was so amused to hear of your jumping the laurels in the garden. Louis told me that at the thought of the wedding you cleared the bushes in great style. I wonder what the Barley people will think of their new Curate and his wife if they see us both flying over the hedges and ditches in our glee. Sometimes I find it hard to keep my spirits in bounds. I let off steam by singing now and then. Mother and Isabella are coming to stay with me for a few days – it will be very nice for me, for I shall have someone to let off steam to and speak about my Agnes. There is to be a concert at Westbury given by the Taylors on Wednesday. Herbert and Agnes are going to sing – in fact it was for them it was got up. I am going to sleep at Jack's, as there is no spare room in their house. I had an hour's sleep in my arm-chair after coming away from the vicarage and feel much fresher for it. Now, dear pet, I must finish as I must answer your Father and Mother's kind invitation. So with fondest love and kisses – I wish I could have one.

He is her own,
ARTHUR

Colston Parade, 12 August 1881

My Own One,

You would have laughed had you been here yesterday. I went in to the Vicarage and had a hard game of tennis with the Norris's. Hugh and I beat Edward and Frank. Then we tried high jumping. The vicar and a Rev Canon who came to see St Mary's with a view to filling my place, looked on. I and Edward beat the rest and

I was even with Edward. The vicar also joined in the fun and Mr C made a feeble attempt. Then we tried long jump. Hugh and I were best at this and I fancy I got an inch or so further than he did. Mrs Norris and Mrs Claxton were also much interested in the sport. Then we tried hop-step-and-jump; Edward was best at this, winning by a foot. The next variety was a race three times round the house, handicap; Edward had a long start but came to grief round the corner. Frank being the two mile runner at school started scratch and Hugh and I even. Frank gave up and left Hugh and I on the field and Hugh having got the start of me there was no passing so I gave up. Then we had a three-legged race – Edward and I went first rate but there was no room for a regular race and so we contented ourselves with cantering round the lawn. It was then time to go into dinner or I do not know when we should have stopped. After dinner we had some rough sort of music. Oh, how I did long for you to be there to play the accompaniments. Then we tried some more feats with our little feet and hands till prayers were announced. Today I am quite stiff with the result of such exercises.

About the groomsmen, we are certain of Francis, Herbert, Willie, Geo Layard and Fred Wilde. Will you think of someone to ask and in case Alfred Evans fails at the last, can you get a second. I won't forget about the certificate of banns, dear, but she may as well remind him of it just before he leaves here in case I should do so.

Darling, he does not like to think of her in low spirits, she seemed to be so from saying that the others laughed and had fun but it made her feel all the more dull. How I wish I could come and cheer you up and give you a kiss. Oh, I do so long to have a sweet embrace. Can't you come back with Jack for a few days. No I suppose you can't, as you are going into residence unless you put off the banns for another week. Oh, wouldn't it be sweet to see you again if only for an hour. But, dear, I must not propose impossibilities, we must have patience, hard tho' it is. Darling, I hardly know what to think about her going to the picnic; I am glad she had said 'no' and I am sorry. Glad to think she really does not care to go with men, showing how truly she has given her entire self to him and sorry because it might have cheered her up a bit; a little change and diversion might have done her good. She must keep her spirits up, dear, for his sake, be cheerful, love because you are happy; if we are separated for a short time, dear, don't be miserable else people will think you are unhappy and repent the step you have taken; this thought keeps me up; thinking of you, sweet one, is the greatest happiness I have now, to possess you will be greater bliss still for, darling one, I love you so dearly that nothing short of your own self can satisfy my longing heart.

I have had another present from an unexpected source. Salvini, the Italian living here, gave me two plaster frames with white plaster figures inside – curious and pretty. Would you rather go to an hotel in town or into lodgings? I could see about them when I went to Barley. Fancy in 35 days we shall be *man and wife* – Oh, you Darling!

With his fondest love,
He is her own,
ARTHUR

Colston Parade, 13 August 1881

My Own One,

I hope she is feeling in better spirits, her letter this morning made me think you were; try to get something to amuse you as the twilight draws the curtains over the sky, don't let your sunny nature decline, because the sun himself retires. If thinking and brooding over me and the wedding makes you feel in the dumps all I say is, don't think of me; that is a very bold and daring thing for me to say but it will show you how sure I feel of your love. Nothing I like more than to know you think about me but, darling, she will understand what he means when he says do not sit down by yourself and brood over things, for I don't know what you will hatch. She will quite think that he is calling her an old chicken and probably will feel quite offended; well, dear, it is better to be an old and experienced chicken than a young one, who can trust to herself, though perhaps she would rather be the latter and have trust in him and be an obedient little person.

Now to business, dear one. I will tell Sister Julia that we both would prefer that she gave us glass and will go out and get it when I hear from her again. The presents are coming in fast now, dear; I wish she would make out a list of the presents received and promised then we could see what we are still in want of, keep a copy herself and send one to me and add anything you think we shall want, then I may suggest that such are our wants when asked.

I am glad you seem to have got a servant girl you like and I suppose I ought not to grumble at £12 a year; how is it Jack managed to get one for so much less, they seem to do things very comfortably for them; but of course, darling, I must leave this with you knowing more about it but if you can get a good one, a useful general servant for less, of course you will do so. I am grieved to hear your mother's back is so bad. Tell her to take the greatest care of herself, for we want her to be quite strong and well by this time next month. As for Bella, if she does not get well by the wedding I don't know what we ought not to do to her. I must try and think of some dreadful torture to put her to if she does not recover before then.

Now, darling, I must go out. I could sit and think about her for the rest of the afternoon but then I should be neglecting my duty which would displease her, he knows, so with best love and hopes that soon he will get the locket.

He is her own true,
Arthur

My Darling One,

I must at once ask you to forgive me for not writing by the 5 o'clock post and I think you will when I explain how it is. I started off this morning by the 10 o'clock train with many others to Christian Malford for the funeral of Archdeacon Randall. When we alighted I found one of the choir boys with an awful cut across his nose and forehead which was occasioned by the sudden stoppage of the train. I at once took him off into the town and had it plastered up. When we returned we found the break which was to conduct us to Christian Malford, had gone; so we had to wait till the next train came in to get a lift in the carriage of some one going there which we did and arrived just in time to join in the procession. Our choir took the services and chanted the psalms and sang 3 hymns. It was a most impressive service and many big men had their eyes full of tears; the Bishop read the lesson and the prayers over the grave. Mrs Randall bore it in a most noble way. After the service we all went and had some lunch and got to Chippenham to catch the 5.15 train which did not leave till 5.40, too late, dear One, to catch the post he ought to have written by. She will see, dear, how impossible it was; I had intended coming back by the 3.25 but all the choir remained and they wanted me to stay with them, and also I was so hungry that I felt I could not return without something to eat. I am afraid, dear, she will be disappointed tomorrow morning. I don't know whether you have a midday post on Sunday; I hope you have. I had better direct this to the Vicarage. Oh darling, how I did laugh at my invitation to the wedding this morning. I don't know why it should have tickled my fancy so; it made me have a very queer feeling seeing our two names together. I have just heard from Mr Barnes to say he had received my letters; he is at Barley, how he does fly about. I sent him the money to the National Bank, Whitby, and wondered why I had no answer, now I hear he is at Barley and has to send for the money to Whitby. He says the swing door leading to the kitchen is included in the valuation; this is very nice for I quite expected to have to pay £4 for it. I also had a letter from Alfred Evans to say he *cannot* come, the *wretch*! He cannot get away from his teaching, after waiting all this time, too; will you provide two men, dear, for I cannot see my way to asking any others, three having failed – Jendwine, Dandy and Evans. This morning I received a small parcel tied up with white satin ribbon and I said at once, hurrah, here is the locket and I opened it to find a piece of wedding cake and you may imagine my disappointment better than I can express it. The cake was from a cousin in town who was married on the 10th. When do you think, dear, the locket will be ready? I am so impatient. When I returned tonight I was dying for my tea and said to Mrs C, 'Oh, get me my tea!' but Mr C said she was gone out for the evening and he did not know how to lay my tea so I thought I would go and see Jack but he had not returned tho' expected every minute. Mr Sampson asked me to come in and I went and had a capital tea but Jack had not turned up when I came away at 8. The bells are now ringing a muffled peal for the Archdeacon. Just had a letter from Mrs Norris to ask me to breakfast with her to meet Mr Bish, I suppose a candidate for Redcliffe and to take him to school. Dear One, it is now 9 o'clock and I have to finish my sermon for tomorrow so must draw to a close. I shall long to hear all about you from Jack. I suppose you are now seated at the vicarage. I hope, darling, she will not be very angry and disappointed at not getting this when she expected, she will see that he could not help it. And now, darling, good night, with his fondest love

He is her own,

ARTHUR

P.S. My cards are printed:

Rev. A. J. Thorndike but I think I shall have them altered. Do you like Rev. Arthur T . . . or Rev. Arthur J. T . . . or Rev. Arthur J. W. T . . .?

My Very Dearest One,

Your letter was so sweet this morning, it has made me feel happy all day. I am not worthy of such true love as yours, dear, though I should deeply mind if I did not know that it was sincere and true. I only hope, dear one, I shall not disappoint you as an husband. I constantly pray for strength to act up to the new position I am about to enter upon, and be a faithful and true one to you, dear love. I am very glad to hear that Mr & Mrs Strange are going to honour us by their presence at Barley, it will be very nice to see them. I wonder what they will think of our home; they won't come till we have got it all nice and comfortable. How I wish I could have sat in the drawing room last Sunday and heard you playing; you will play sacred music to me at Barley, dear, on Sundays, won't you? How delightful it will be after the day's work is done to sit down with her and listen to her playing sweet music; it will be like being in heaven. I suppose I may expect the locket now in a few days. I am longing to see it, dear; I know I shall like it, especially if it has a good likeness of my Agnes in it; her own gift and her own dear face in it, how I shall prize it!! Mother has been very busy all the morning marking my new things, my trousseau, and Isabella has covered the two frames Salvini gave me with velvet and they look much more handsome. Tomorrow we are all going to the concert at Westbury. I wish you were coming, darling. I shall have an opportunity of talking about you to them all which will be very charming. I like Mother and Isabella being here so much for that reason that I can have some one to talk of you to. He had a letter from Frank this morning and he says he is flying about the country evicting unfortunates from their dwellings because they won't pay. What disagreeable work. Miss Parnell was most active and Frank says 'Don't you think it would be a good plan if I arranged to marry Miss Parnell on the same day as you are to be married', she would make an active wife for she can jump hedges and ditches without any trouble which might be convenient for an officer's wife.

With fondest and best love,
He is her own,
ARTHUR

My Own Darling One,

I am so truly grateful for the beautiful locket, it is indeed a handsome one. Mother and Isabella think it is a little large but it is because I have never worn a locket that it looks large. Shan't I prize it for your dear sake. The photos I think are dreadful. Neither of them are really good enough to go in the beautiful locket; they do not do justice to my sweet Agnes. Why not have the one we had done in Bristol made smaller – either your man could do it, or I could take it to Midwinter to have it done. I have got the locket on and feel most proud of it. I return the photos, dear one, as not worthy of her dear self. I don't know why you did not get a letter yesterday morning by the first post for I posted it by 5.30. I am very sorry, dear. We are all just off to Westbury for the concert. I hope it will be a success.

Have you decided anything more about the servant? The one you mention seems to answer requirements. He hopes, dear, she will not have all her dresses made as tight as the one in the photo – I think it is much too tight. With his fondest love,

He is still her own true,
ARTHUR

Colston Parade, 18 August 1881

My Own One,

We have just finished dinner and the two Evans, Chrissie and Clary, are here. They are going to see the church. Darling One,

107

I cannot express in words how I like the locket. It is a beauty; only I shall like it very much better when it has got my dear One's likeness in it. When will she send him one to put in it. Mother and Jack and I went to see about the dinner service this morning. The pattern is very pretty; 60 pieces for £1. 7 shillings. Jack has the list now but I hope to get it to send it with this letter. I also decided on the glass, £5. 5, a very handsome one. Jack and Louis are very much taken with it and I expect they will sell the one they have and get one like the one I have chosen. Jack offered me his glass for £3. 15, half the price he gave for it, as part of their wedding present but I think the glass would not stand in our room and I do not like it so well as the one I have chosen, so he will have to sell it if he wants to change it. It was very kind to offer it to us and if it would have fitted I think I would have been tempted to close with the offer; I have been looking at some stuff to make a nice dressing gown, for I thought you would not like me to appear before you without a dressing gown.

Another thing, dear, I have been thinking about, which has not occupied much of my thoughts before; that is, don't you think, dear, it would be much pleasanter to go to Hastings or Dover or some seaside place than going to London. I think myself, it would be infinitely more pleasant. In the first place London is a most doleful sort of place to go to, especially in September when nothing is going on and there is no novelty to either of us to go there and there are so many friends about town whom we should be bound to go and see, though I should not care at all to do so, nor do I think she would. Whereas at Hastings or Dover we should have *novelty* – no *friends* and good sea air. The hotel would cost about the same as in town and we could go to the theatre there as well as in town. I do not think we should find it any more expensive and to my mind much more enjoyable, but, dear one, I feel I am very selfish in saying all this, if you have thoroughly made up your mind that our honeymoon must be in London. We should pass through town from either of these places to go to Royston so that we could see about the piano and stores on our way back. I have just remembered that I totally forgot to send you the book for the [Army & Navy] Stores. What a forgetful fellow I am. Will you care to have me, dear one, now that you have experienced my weakness? Shall I send the book of prices at the Stores? Don't you think, dear, the fresh sea air would be much more beneficial to both of us than smoky, dingy, London air. Write and tell me what you think about it. I can't help thinking you will like it better. I wish I could afford to give you a fur cloak, dear, but I can't.

The concert went off very well and we were such a family party, and, dear one, she was the topic of much of the conversation which was the most pleasant part for him.

Thanking her a thousand times for her splendid gift of the locket.

He is more than ever,
Her loving,
ARTHUR

Colston Parade, 19 August 1881

My Very Dearest One,

I am afraid from your letter this morning that I did not make you understand how *very much* I liked the locket. I am, dear one, perfectly pleased with it and when it has your dear face in it I shall like it even better still. I have cut [out] the head of that photo of yours in the dark hat – it is rather too large for the locket, but I like the expression of your sweet face in that photo, and now I shall be able to look at you whenever I like and if this gives me delight, oh, what will be the joy of always having the living Agnes to look at and talk to. I wonder what she thought of his letter today about not going to London for our honeymoon. I cannot but think we should enjoy ourselves more at a lively seaside place than in the empty streets of London – at least London never looks so lively out of season. So I vote we do not go to Town. What does she think? Poor little woman, she quite felt he had been finding fault with her dressing, when she considers herself such a stylish person. The photo gave the appearance that your dress was so much tighter than when she was in Bath but as she says it is the same dress it must have been my fancy; you see, dear, how he notices, and sometimes picks her to pieces. He hopes she can bear a little chaff, being a slave, as I suppose all girls are, to fashion. Well, dear, the only thing I hope is you won't have your dresses as tight as some do that if they fall down cannot get up again. You will say, 'I shall always have my husband to pick me up if I fall down' but you must always manage to do so, if at all, when he is by.

Now, sweet one, to business and put aside chaffings. Had she not better go to the photographers who did the photo you sent me and sit again, for he will change you for the ones you have had done, which do not do justice to my angel. One was certainly better than the other but neither were good enough for her, dear. If he does not succeed with another, then we can try somewhere else but I should like to have a nice one of you, the proper size, before the Wedding Day. I sent them back at once that no time might be lost in having another done. He does hope she was not annoyed at his sending them back so sharp.

Darling, I am so glad to hear you are happy at the vicarage, it will help you to bear the trial of separation and you will not get so down in the dumps. Oh! I wish I could run in and cheer you up when you are so low-spirited. Keep up your spirits, dear love. It is only a little more than 3 weeks. Oh, what joy! Dear one, I hardly know sometimes what to do next with so much to do before I leave here, and sermons and I seem to be rushed all day long. Write, dear, and say exactly what you would like with regard to where we go for our honeymoon – your wish shall be mine, sweet love, so only say and I will go, even if it is to the moon (provided there is anything to take us). And now, dear, I must do some visiting. Goodbye and with his fondest love,

He is her own, true,
ARTHUR

My Own One,

I was so glad to get your letter this morning and to find that it is
no disappointment to you to give up going to spend our honeymoon in Town. I like the idea of Folkestone quite as much as
Dover or Hastings and if we found it dull at Folkestone we
could go to Dover. But, dear, I do not see the necessity of going
to London to go to Folkestone. I have not looked out the trains
but I should have thought it would be much quicker to go by
the coast line thro' Brighton. Will you look it out, dear, and see
which will be the shortest journey. It would be much nicer to
get the journey over the first day and not have to start off again
next day. Now, sweet one, don't be nervous about me and think
I am ill, for I am not. For the last day or two the weather has
been very trying and with a good deal of parish work on hand I
was a little done up; I have not been able to get my breakfast till
9 o'clock every morning and the waiting so long for it made me
feel sick and I couldn't eat it when it came, but now, dear one,
I always have a few biscuits with my cup of milk and I feel
alright and ready for breakfast. I thought, dear one, it would not
do any good telling you of such trifling ailments for it would
only make you feel anxious. I could almost wish to be seedy
enough to bring you here to see me but I must put away such a
selfish wish. It will not be for much longer. Fancy in a little more
than three weeks we shall be together, never to be parted more,

> 'For all I dare and do
> Shall be alone for you
> At your dear feet I'll lay it sweet
> My life's whole work for you.'

So, Darling, you need not fear that as long as I have strength I
will use it to protect you and to work for you. If only you knew
how strong I am you would not talk of having to tread your
weary path alone, for I expect I shall live longer than you dear,
but we need not look forward to any sad future. God knows what

is best for us both and He will not allow us if we both trust in Him to take any step unsanctioned by His gracious will. I do feel so thankful for His help. I really sometimes wonder at myself for the things I am enabled to do thro' His Grace assisting me. For instance, yesterday I was occupied all day with various duties and the Thorndikes and the Taylors came down to tea, that I had no time to prepare my sermon for the evening services except ¾ hour before going into Church and, dear one, I asked the Holy Spirit to inspire my mouth with wisdom that I might speak words of understanding and I went with such a delightful feeling of confidence that I preached without any difficulty.

Oh, dear, how I did laugh about the black beetle – how horrified you must have been, I am sure I should have shrieked; of all things in the live stock I hate beetles the most, though they are such wonderful creatures. How glad you must have been to have woken up after your dreams. I was in the same condition the other night, only it was a robber breaking into the house and I went up to him and said, "Oh, you have mistaken the house, let me show the house you want," so I walked him out and took him to the Police Station – then I woke.

We are going out to make some Clifton calls and leave p.p.c. cards. Mrs Norris has just sent me a picture of Redcliffe Church and floating dock beautifully framed in gilt. They leave here on Wednesday. I see Mother has been writing to you – I hope to tell you I am not so bad as she seems to have made me out. Dear One, I am so happy and longing for Thursday three weeks. Mr Dickerson will publish my banns on Sunday, as Jack will be at the Mission Church. With fondest love to her dear self and kind remembrances to Mr & Mrs Strange,

He is her own,
ARTHUR

P.S. Do, Dear, have another photo taken for the locket.

My Own Dearest One,

I was so delighted to get your letter this morning telling me you were better. I was not the least shocked at your taking brandy. If I had been there I should have done the same, for it is the best medicine for the complaint. Do take care of yourself, dearest, I dare say it will really do you good when it is over. How fortunate your having it before the wedding. Don't go and get another attack. I have just had a letter from Mother saying I can get a lovely bouquet in Bath, quite as good as those from Covent Garden and cheaper. We can bring it between us when we come this day three weeks, so there will be no fear of your not getting it in time. Oh, darling, I can hardly contain my joy when I think of the wedding. How often do I picture my loved Angel coming up the aisle in all her purity and 'the virgins that be her fellows shall bear her company – joy and gladness shall she be brought and shall enter into the King's Temple. Thou art fairer than the children of men, full of grace are thy lips because God hath blessed thee for ever.'

I am very sorry Francis is not to sleep at the Vicarage with me, for he is such fun and would keep my spirits up to the mark, supposing I did feel nervous at being wedded to an angel; he would be able to support me and it would be jolly to chat over things with him the night before. We should not the least mind sleeping in the same room or even in the same bed – we often do it at home. I should like it very much more, if it could be managed without much difficulty, only don't let there be any feelings about it. I know Francis would like it as much as I should to sleep together.

Darling one, I have a very good idea for a bouquet for you. Lilies are very much in the fashion now and sunflowers. Don't you think a large lily as a centre flower and sunflowers all round would look well, or would you prefer instead of sunflowers white peteunias (I don't think that is the way to spell it). I have a very nice one in my garden. There are a few more blossoms coming on which will be ready just in time for the 15th. Darling, I must go out, for I have such a lot to do and a sermon to preach tonight and have nothing ready yet,

So, dear love, with fondest affections,

He is still her own,
ARTHUR

Colston Parade, 21 August 1881

My Own Beloved One,

I was so delighted to get your sweet letter this morning so full of fun. I expected she would soon get tired of him if she takes such trouble over every ailment he may have as she said she would in her letter. Dear one, it has been a most happy day – the services have been most helpful. The Vicar preached in the morning on the Gospel – Christ weeping over Jerusalem and would he weep over our town and over us individually on account of our sins as a people and as simple sinners. Mr Dickerson published our banns this morning service and was a little nervous and stammered over it. I did not feel in the least nervous. I wonder how she got on and whether she felt nervous. I suppose she retired to the vestry. I preached in the afternoon to the children on the question 'Where art thou?'. Mother liked it and thought the children would have liked it. I wish she could have been sitting in Church then she could have given her opinion. She will do so at Barley, won't she, darling? Jack and Louie are here, they are all singing hymns and it sounds very well; they are just finishing 'Onward Christian Soldiers'.

Mr Dickerson gave us a most magnificent sermon on the subject of the Man of God and the old Prophet of Bethel. I often wonder when I hear a good sermon whether I shall ever get the power to do the same. Dear one, how I did laugh at your telling Louie to come and nurse me. I don't know why you should think I am in such a weak and feeble condition. The only illness

I have is pining to see the Angel of my life. I said goodbye to Mrs Norris today as she goes away tomorrow and I don't expect I shall see her again.

She will not get this, dear, by the first post, for it is quite impossible to write before 1 o'clock on Sunday, as you know, dear. I am glad you like the idea of going to the sea instead of London. I vote we get straight to Folkestone without breaking the journey.

Goodnight, dear love,
God keep thee in peace,
Her own fond,
ARTHUR

Redcliffe, 25 August 1881

My One,

By this time three weeks I shall no longer be a lone and miserable bachelor. We shall just have started on our journey: all the ceremony over, and I shall not be sorry when it is, and then, oh, the joy of living together and working together!!

He was glad to hear she was recovering from her attack of biliousness and shall hope to hear tomorrow you are quite your dear self again. Oh, how I shall jump for joy when Wednesday fortnight comes. He has still a good deal to do and arrange before then which will make the time go even quicker. My college friend Tarleton is going to be married here in Redcliffe on the 7th and he has asked me to help tie him up. This will be good practice for me, dear one, won't it, only instead of saying, 'Wilt thou have this woman to be thy wedded wife' I shall have to answer that question myself. I hope I shall not shriek out 'I will' in the joy of my heart because it might not add dignity to the proceedings. I shall hardly be accountable for my action on that morning so don't wonder if I come to Church in my nightgown and new dressing gown. I dare say I should cut a very good figure if I appeared in such a costume. Mother and Isabella are working me a splendid pair of slippers which I could also wear. Oh, darling, how I did laugh about the frills on your nightdress. I should *love* you, sweet one, if you had not a frill or piece of lace in your possession – you *dear* little woman.

He is afraid he has not been much help to her about the dinner service but I should think you could get them quite as cheap in Southampton. I like the pattern Jack has chosen for his set very much and if you cannot get one to please you I should certainly get it here. There is the ordinary £1. 1 set and we could add to that whatever we liked, so if the set at Southampton does not meet your full approbation decide to have the set here.

You ask me what I think of the bouquet – well, knowing you are fond of large things I can order one of the lilies and, if white sunflowers are to be had, can have them put in and then filled up with one or two full blown white roses and a few peteunias supplied from my own garden. Isabella can make an ornamental piece of notepaper to go round it and I think you cannot fail to be pleased with such an aesthetic bouquet. Herbert asked me if we had an afternoon tea-set given us and I have told him yes and have suggested a salad bowl, hot water dish, butter dish or some ornaments for the drawing room mantel piece. I took the silver mustard pot to have the crest put on this morning, it is such a handsome one. Has she had a photo taken for the locket, dear? He does want one so badly. Do have a nice one done. How very nice the letter from Jane is, I only wish we could get such a servant for our cook. Have you decided on the £12 girl, dear? It is such a miserable day – pouring with rain. I shall not mind at Barley what the weather is, for there will be always sunshine at home.

> With fondest love, he considers himself,
> her own,
> ARTHUR

My Own Dearest One,

I cannot make out why you did not get my letter by the midday post. I posted it here on Sunday evening. You will receive the certificate of banns this morning so your mind will be at rest on that score. The choir are going to Cheddar this morning in about $\frac{1}{2}$ an hour so you must not mind a short letter today. I shall ask Mrs Carter to post it by 5.30. On the £12 servant you have not said anything more about it so I do not know what you have done. What do you think about the girl I mentioned to you – would you care to have her? Do you think it would be a bad thing for Elizabeth – only she need never know it. It would depend very much on the girl herself. If she is *really* penitent, coming to us might be the very best thing for her. Write and tell me what you think. There is not much time to lose if you have not got a servant girl yet. Dickerson gave us the mustard pot and I have the crest on it – solid silver – it is very good of him.

Now, dear love, I must fly off or shall lose my seat,

So with best and fondest love,
He is her own
ARTHUR

Redcliffe, 31 August 1881

Darling One,

This will be the last time you will ever be able to say that on August 31 'I am Miss Bowers'. This month will never see you again under that title. Fancy, dear, only 15 more days.

We had a long and pleasant day yesterday to Cheddar. We started at 10 with a coach and a break, each with four horses. I rode on the coach box with Dickerson and had a very good view of the country. Coming back I went with the boys in the break and we had singing and I told them stories nearly all the way, which kept them very quiet. We got back at 10. We had dinner at Cox's and, fancy, the dear one had been there and he not there and then he went there and she was absent. Oh, what fun he would have had if she had been with him. He will not be lonely much longer, and won't this 'child' lead her a life. Doesn't she often tremble to think what a tyrant he will be. Well, dear, it came on to pour while we were having our food but luckily cleared after.

I expect Herbert has sent the salad bowl; it was one of the things I mentioned to him. I do not think Francis would like us to put by any of his present. He seems to want to give us a handsome present with the money but I shall see him on Saturday and I hope we can arrange something. The music stand is a good idea. I am getting so excited about the wedding that sometimes I hardly know whether I am on my head or my heels. I went on Monday to Bath to see the dress and I think it is most handsome. At first I did not care about the two balloon shaped excrescences behind; but, after, I thought them becoming. Won't they all look sweet, but the sweetest of all will be my pure and lovely Agnes. I wish I could write better letters, dear, but I can hardly give my mind to any one thing for there are so many to think about.

With fondest and best love,
He is her own,
ARTHUR

Colston Parade, 2 September 1881

Beloved One,

This day fortnight we shall be just starting for London feeling very queer, I have no doubt, with heaps of rice down our backs and our hearts overflowing with love and gratitude. You will be feeling sad at leaving your parental roof where every comfort and happiness has been yours; where you have been made so much of as you so richly deserve; where high, low, rich and poor loved you. Darling, you will be leaving all this for love of me. I often wonder at your love and think how *true* it is, to be able to give up so much to 'Come and live with me and be my love'. Sweet one, I will try and make you happy and have found thro' life that what one tries hard to do is generally successful, so I have no fear that we shall not be perfectly happy in each other's love. Oh, how often do I picture our home at Barley with the dear Wife to brighten it. I often sing 'Of all the wives as e'er you know there's none like my Agnes I trow' and whenever I come in from my day's work I shall find 'Agnes's face to bless the place and welcome me' and my prayer will be 'A long long life to my sweet wife and I shall trouble any body to find a mate as sweet as my Agnes – Yeo Ho, lad, Yeo Ho – The parson's wife, the parson's star shall be'.

Now, dear love, to business, as she so sweetly expresses it. I have written about the servant girl and expect an answer to-morrow and then I shall be able to judge whether we ought to take her or not. I mentioned it to Mother and she strongly advises me not to take her. If you have engaged one, that decides the matter, and I only trust she will prove a faithful and true one. Elizabeth has grown since she has been at the Paragon and looks very happy and is learning her work well.

Dear one, is it your wish that the groomsmen should wear white ties and gloves? Because I must write and tell them or they may wear coloured which, as Willie suggests, might not be in keeping with the dresses. I did not say anything about the dresses in my Tuesday letter because I had to fly off so quickly for the Cheddar trip and I had not time to collect my thoughts on the subject. I think dear Isabella's is lovely – it wants a little alteration to make it fit exactly. How well they will all look and how proud I shall feel at having a bride with such a goodly train of virgins following after her; the baskets will give a very pretty contrast to the white dresses and I should think some scarlet flower on the shoulder, the left side, would be very becoming. What a quantity of presents we are getting. Willie's will remind me of college days as well as of him when I am in my study.

And so, dear love, I must finish, for I must go and do some visiting.

With fondest love,
He is her own,
ARTHUR

My Beloved Agnes,

How I did devour your letter in bed this morning. Last night I felt the symptoms of a heavy cold so I put my feet in hot water and did not get up for Matins but devoured your letter over my breakfast. I think I have mastered the cold by doing this, tho' I feel very seedy now. I shall be alright tomorrow. How I have thought of my loved one last night and this morning. Fancy dear, this day fortnight will be our first day together as man and wife. I hope it will be warmer than it is now, tho' we can hardly expect it at the sea-side. She shall do just as she likes about staying in town the first night and going to the theatre. After the excitement of the day she might find the journey to Folkestone too long and tedious. I do not mind which you do; it comes really to this, whether you prefer the trouble of unpacking in town with the fun of going to the theatre or the trouble of another railway journey and no repacking and no theatre. Now just do whichever you like best and that will please me best. It will be very jolly having a talk in the train and it will be very jolly going to the theatre.

Now about the servant. I enclose the letters about her and from her. One was written to home. She is highly recommended and if she would come for £8. 0 a year I should be very strongly inclined to take her. If we did, I feel she would be a good servant, for we should have a hold upon her at once. If it had not been for her sin she would not come for £8. 0 and perhaps she may not now, but I should not offer her as much as to one who was not

120

in the same position. I do not think she would be likely to tell Elizabeth anything about it and of course we never should. Write and tell me at once what you think if you have not decided with the £12 girl. I feel it is a clergyman's place to help the fallen if it is in his power but must also consider the effects likely to be produced.

Frank has applied for leave from the 9th to the 24th and will be with me on the 10th. Do you think it is likely I could come up and see you at the expense of my dinner – Mr Bodge would say 'your future wife will keep but your dinner will spoil if kept and then there is so much good food gone'. Shall I take Mr Bodge's advice and have my dinner and then come up with the rest to see you? How very likely!! No, dear one, nothing shall keep us longer apart than can possibly be helped and if I never had any more dinner again I should come to you first. What a jolly chat we will have. Oh, the idea of telling you tales all night. Do you know, directly I lay my head on my pillow I go to sleep and so if you expect me to amuse you with curtain lectures I shall have to practice doing so in my sleep. Shan't I go to sleep sharp on the night of the 15th after all the previous excitement. You must talk to me and tell me tales to keep me awake. Jack and I are going to pay calls this afternoon.

So, with fondest love and kisses sweet,
He remains her true,
ARTHUR

Colston Parade, 4 September 1881

My Own Dearest One,

I sent off this morning a box with a few of the presents I have received. In the box are an inkstand with pen and pencil from Jendwine, serpentine marble salt cellars from Mr and Mrs Langford, Vicar of Bere Regis, a silver mustard pot and spoon from Mr Dickerson, an asparagus spoon from Geo Layard. He feels very grateful for all the presents we are receiving. It makes me love her so for saying what she did about the crest. Then, she thinks, having said a sweet thing she can ask him anything else she likes. Well, dear one, she has asked him a rather a difficult thing. You ask me 'to promise that if anything happens to you not to let another woman touch your things'. Well, I don't know how I am to manage while we are enjoying our honeymoon, for certainly it would not do to take all your presents to Folkestone and if we do not, I cannot promise that no other woman shall touch them. But, dear one, she must not think so badly of her sex for I cannot bring myself to believe that a woman's touch has anything so defiling in it as to spoil that which belongs to another. He thinks that as she contemplates having a good score out of him he had better get another out of her first, then he will be two to the good. As for a second wife why, dear, I have heard of many who have two wives living but I promise you that I will not do this. As long as you are alive no one else shall claim me as husband: and darling, putting jokes aside, I do not think any woman but your dear self will ever be able to call me her husband. Your love is too true and genuine to be easily or *ever* forgotten: so don't trouble your head about any future Mrs Arthur Thorndike.

Darling, I must tell you of a little disappointment I had this morning. I did not get up for Matins, how lazy I am getting! And when I heard the postman's knock I said, 'Now for a letter from my sweet one' but to my surprise only one letter was shoved under my door and I could see at a glance it was not your handwriting. I was puzzling over the reason of it when I heard the postman's knock again and this time, oh joy, he brought your dear letter. Darling, I was so glad to hear you had a desk given to you for it will be for her own use and it will be delightful to see the dear little housewife with her Russian leather desk! What a splendid lot of presents she is getting. It shows how she is beloved. But there is one who loves her dearer than all and he alone can sign himself,

Her own true,
ARTHUR

122

My Very Dearest One,

I think I have mastered the cold in my head. Yesterday I was afraid I was in for bronchitis but today all the symptoms of that are gone and I have not coughed once today. I am feeling a little tired after the services but I expect I shall be as right as ever tomorrow. I suppose I caught the cold coming from Cheddar. You don't think that my being married to you could make me feel excited? Such an everyday occurrence! He is quite making out that she is nobody and she, of course, believes it will!

I must write off at once about the servant and get her if I can. I should think under the circumstances she would be glad to come for £8.

Next Sunday will be my last here. I am to preach in the afternoon to the children – I am rather glad.

What ornaments do the bridesmaids intend wearing? Silver or gold? I should think silver would be best and do they intend wearing a flower in their hair for the evening? They ought all to do the same. Let me know or tell Isabella. I saw Isabella's hat again last night and think it is splendid – such good taste – so simple and so good for it becomes her very well. This is not at all the sort of conversation for Sunday, dear, but she must forgive him for there is not much time to decide the little points of dress. So delighted to hear of all the presents and now good-bye loved one.

With many kisses,
He remains her true,
ARTHUR

P.S. About the party, dear – she must do what she thinks right. I shall not mind, for my trust is in you and I know you love me too dearly to do anything to displease me. If you think you ought to go do so by all means.

My Dearest Angel,

She cannot think dear how miserable he has been today and yesterday though I feel I quite deserved the scolding you gave me. I did long to hear you say you had forgiven me. Today when your letter arrived at 12 o'clock I thought Ah, now I shall have the word of comfort and forgiveness but I was doomed to suffer still longer, and your letter instead of removing my pain, deepened it, for I could not help fancying, and I suppose it was only fancy, that there was not the same warmth of love and affection in your letter. I do not for one moment doubt that you love me as well as ever but, dear one, I suppose when you wrote it you had not read my letter in answer to your scolding, but it seems to me such ages ago that I wrote it, whereas in reality I suppose you only got it this morning. You do not say a word about how your throat is. I hope it is no worse. You promised you would tell me everything about yourself, so mind you tell me when you are not well. I feel anxious to know how you are, dear; it pains him to know she is ill and more than ever when she does not say a word about it. Oh, dear, how that sentence of yours did cut me 'What are you going to do on bank holiday – if anything too sweet don't say a word about it'. It is the first time she has asked him to hide anything from her. Oh, I do hope it does not indicate that you do not trust me. No, I will not let such a thought remain in my mind. I believe and trust you, dear, and till I have proofs to the contrary I will believe the same of you. Darling one, I have sent you just a little token of my deep and sincere love and affection for you in the shape of a little prayer book. I did not observe that you had one, so I send you one and if she can find any use for it she will do so for the sake of the one who would die for her sake.

Dear one, I have to be very careful to make my money do till the 15th and to pay all my bills. I think I shall just about manage it and have about £1 in hand after paying everything; then after I leave here I shall get my quarter's allowance from the Vicar and at the beginning of October from Mother. This will have somehow to last until Christmas. I ordered my banker to draw the £200 from the 3 a/c which will cost me £1.5 so I shall have £18.15 left for expenses of the move and other items at leaving here. You won't have a rich husband to start with. I have not heard from Mr Barnes so that I cannot send the cheque till I know where to send it. I wrote to Mr Gordon again today and explained about the servants and said we would try James for a few months by the week at 10/- and see how we could afford it. There are some very nice pier glasses in black and gold with two shelves for 45/- and 30/-. Sister Julia asked me if she should give us that instead of spoons. I said no, the latter were more useful and I dare say someone will give us a glass. Would your friend who offered us a clock like to give this instead, as there is a clock promised. Darling, her prayer was beautiful. I did pray when I had read it that it might be fully answered. To my mind you are too pure and holy for me; I am not good enough to have such a sweet one to take care of and I pray that, as God has granted me my petition in giving me one for my wife who had the fear and love of God in her heart, he will make me more holy and enable to support and comfort and not pain the wife of my bosom. About Canon Damer, dear, I did not know that Mr Owen was also going to help in the service. It would be very difficult to squeeze in a fourth I should think and as I have not yet asked him I think with you I had better not. Canon Venables perhaps may be able to come on the 15th, I must write and find out. He said it would give him much pleasure to do so if he could. I have a temperance meeting in about 10 minutes so I must say goodbye, dear love. How I long for a letter tomorrow. I have paid dearly for my joking.

> With fondest love and a hug of affection,
> He is still
> Her Own True
> ARTHUR

Colston Parade, 5 September 1881

My Own One,

I can only write a short letter to her today as I am so full of work I hardly know what to do next. I have written to Miss Caswell about Caroline Beavis and offered her £9. I thought as she was a good servant and had been 5 years in one place I would say £9 instead of £8. I should not mind giving a little more but shall see what she says to the £9. I said I would probably increase her wages after a year if she suited. I put clearly before her the risk I was taking in having a girl in her position in our house and therefore could not offer her as much as I could to another who was not in the same condition. I am thinking of getting an oak and silver waiter with F's money and also a dumb waiter for the table. I went in with Jack and his belongings to Claxton's last night and had such a pleasant evening. Tonight we are going to Mr Lawson's to hear an Italian play. I hope to get him for the C.E.F.S. meeting tomorrow night.

> With sweetest love to my Own Darling One,
> He remains her,
> ARTHUR

P.S. Who have you got for the two extra groomsmen?

Colston Parade, 6 September 1881

My Beloved One,

Only 9 days more – what joy! I am afraid, dear one, she did not get his letter by the first post this morning as I fear I was just too late to catch the 5.30 clearing. Tomorrow I shall feel very queer taking part in the marriage ceremony of Frank Tarleton and Miss Roberts. I shall be picturing to myself how much sweeter my angel will look next week and how much happier I shall feel. Both yesterday and today I have been ringing marriage peals and the ringers want very much to ring a peal on the 15th. I suppose I shall get an answer from the servant tomorrow but I would not send off the one you have thought of taking till I hear from Caroline Beavis or else we may be stranded. Of course, dear love, we will stay in town the first night if she wishes it; how angry I should have been with myself if we had gone on, and you would have preferred staying in town. If I write on Monday to Charing X and to the Pavilion Hotel it will be in plenty of time. I thought the salts handsome – sorry you don't care for them. Of course they do not want insides. I have two meetings tonight of the C.E.F. Senor Pansani is coming to play the zither. Darling, I must be off – the afternoon is flying by – so with fondest love,

He is her own,
ARTHUR

Colston Parade, 7 September 1881

My Very Dearest One,

I have received a letter this morning from Miss Caswell about Caroline Beavis and she declines my offer. She was offered £23 a year which I consider most exorbitant and I am of the opinion that it is wrong to give a girl in her fallen condition such high wages. In the present day the sin of adultery is smoothed over. People say 'Poor thing she has had a misfortune'. She gets much more sympathy and condolence than she did before she sinned. To my mind it is encouraging this sin. I should like to write a strong letter to Miss Caswell on the subject but I don't suppose it would do much good. I must deliberate over it. Of course I shall write and tell her that £12 would be the utmost I should give and as I could get a pure girl for that I would prefer doing so. Will you take the servant you have tried or wait to get another? I was so pleased with the letter from your class and I shall value very much the stick, it being connected so closely with your dear one. I don't mean to say you are a stick or that I shall give you the stick but the giver thro' his love to you has thought of me. Do thank him most warmly for me. Must be off to the wedding. This day week shall be starting for another.

With love and kisses,
He is her own,
ARTHUR

Colston Parade, 7 September 1881

My Own One,

There have been two weddings this morning in the Church. One was supposed to be at 9.30 and the second at 10, but as the first did not arrive till 9.50 the second had to wait. The first was of the grand style, though only a salt merchant, the bride wore a white silk dress with a very long train and had four or five bridesmaids. My friend had a much quieter affair. His bride was dressed in a dark velvet bodice and light petticoat and bonnet to match the dress and no bridesmaids. They did not seem to understand how to go through the service a bit. The steps of the North Gate were literally covered with rice. I went to the breakfast and thought it rather a slow one. I gave the bridegroom a good handful of rice just as they went off. Oh, how it made me think of next week. A girl has just been to me from Jack to enquire about a situation. She has been a housemaid in a clergyman's family and has helped the cook. She got £12. I rather like the look of her – she is only 19 and not confirmed. I am going up this afternoon to see her character at the office.

Last night I had the Temperance Meeting. The children's one was very full and the adults came in pretty good numbers. Mrs Francombe spoke at both about me in a very kind way and they all gave me three hearty cheers and three much heartier ones for the future Mrs Thorndike.

I must not write more, dear, so with deepest love, He is her own,

ARTHUR

My cold is quite well, dear one.

Colston Parade, 8 September 1881

My Darling One,

He is so pleased, dear, to hear of the many and handsome presents she is receiving and he has also had another in the shape of a very handsome Dresden china dish richly embossed in gold from Mrs Norton. I have been on the look out all the morning for Frank. I received a telegram this morning to say he would be here at 9 a.m. but he has not yet turned up. I cannot think why. Bush, my successor, arrived last night and he is now waiting for me to take him round my district to induct him. I think he will be much liked here. I have been told he is very like me. How lucky you did not see him before me or you might never have been Mrs T . . . and how could I have existed any more without you, dear. I don't think I really could now. Life would not be worth living for, without you to share its joys and sorrows. The servant I spoke of yesterday will not come so far away from home as Barley so he must fall back upon the one you have got and with such a manager as my one is will turn her out a good servant. My things will go on Tuesday and I shall write to Barley for Vines to meet them. About how much will you have? Now, dear love, I must go out with Bush. This day week we shall just be starting for London. If she knows any one to get the tickets for the theatre it would perhaps be better than writing for them.

With fondest love,
He is her own true,
ARTHUR

My Own Darling Arthur,

Don't trouble about another servant. I will take the one I have engaged. She will suit us, I expect. I don't think the housemaid you speak of would be at all likely to suit, at least I should not care to risk it, so I will take the one from here. I would much rather. You cannot tell how busy I am today. Marking all my things 'Agnes Thorndike' looks so sweet. I bought you 6 very large bath towels as there were none in the house, also 11 dusters, 6 small towels. We shall not want to use them yet as there are 13 in the house. I bought two new breakfast cloths. We have everything now for our house in the way of silver, except knife rests and sugar tongs. I had nut crackers last night from Mrs Norris. We haven't a hot water jug. These are all things we want. We have a complete set of oak and silver. The tea tray has not arrived yet. Then we have a salad bowl, toast rack, coal scuttle, sugar basin. And in place of the other salad bowl we are going to have a biscuit box and butter dish. Won't our table look sweet when we have any friends. Darling, I must hasten to catch the post. I've been so busy I haven't had time to write much.

> Fondest love and kisses,
> From your own fond,
> AGNES

My Sweet One,

Frank arrived yesterday at 3 looking very well and full of spirits. I went down with him to Bath and spent the evening at home. We had a good talk over the wedding and arrangements. Frank did not quite like the idea of white gloves and ties. He said he had never seen them worn before, and nor have I. Do you think silver grey would look better? There would be nothing of a

flaring contrast in this. What sort of ties ought they to wear –
little ones like those worn for an evening? They would look
rather like waiters but still I do not know what is the correct
thing but I should rather have fancied not white would have
looked best. I have told Geo Layard white but if you think the
grey or lavender would look as well there is plenty of time to
alter it. The servant will not come so far so we must make the
best we can out of the one you have. I had thought of getting one
of the covered hotwater dishes with Frank's money but as you
have two I will not. I think a small canterbury for our music
would be very useful. Also an oak and silver waiter – 25/-. Oh,
darling, how close the time is drawing. I am busy saying goodbye
to everyone and they all wish us health and happiness.

God bless you dear one,

With fondest love, he is her
own ARTHUR

Glen Luie, 10 September 1881

My Darling Arthur,

Just a few lines this morning as I am just going over to Amy's to
make some pastry, etc. About the ties and gloves: tell Francis if
he would rather wear grey to do so. Don't you think they would
be very ugly contrast with the white dresses? White satin ties
are all the fashion now – rather broad bows. All the men had
them on the other night at the dance I went to. I think Alice
Walter and Lilian Harper are coming in for a little while the
night before the wedding just to be introduced so I am going to
write to Mrs Thorndike and tell her I think we will put on
evening dress. Don't let the men do it, though, it doesn't matter
one bit. We thought it would be rather jolly to practise waltzing
for the next night. I will play as much as they like and dance too,
if it won't look undignified. Of course if I see a frown on your
face at my doing such a thing I would of course sit down like a

meek obedient little child and look so penitent. I am afraid I shall never get old in my ways. I do think I frivell a great deal for a married woman that is to be. Well, sweet one, goodbye for the present. I had 3 more painted terracotta plates sent last night.

Fondest love and kisses. Longing to see her own loved one. She is always his very own

AGNES

Glen Luie, 10 September 1881

My Darling Arthur,

I am glad you did not have that housemaid. I think this one here will suit. Of course the girl is rather nervous before our own cook and will do much better, I think, in her own kitchen. The time is drawing rather near now. How do you feel dear? The people here say they have never seen anyone take it so calmly as I do. It is no good exciting oneself about such an everyday affair! I expect I shall like Mrs Morton's dish. I cannot have the crest put on all the silver. The man cannot put it all on under 7 days so we shall send for it the day after the wedding. Then it will be quite ready for Amy to bring. We all went to the Harpers last night and had charades, etc. I didn't care much about it as the young men don't interest me much now. I joined in, though, and made myself as jolly as I could; came home about half past twelve. I suppose Francis is with you now. He seemed to want the brides-maids to go for a sail but they will all leave the house directly we go so I don't see how they can. The Mater's back is still so weak that she will have to rest all the afternoon to be fit for the evening, so the house must be cleared till that time. I hope she will keep up alright. Thank F for his letter – I am longing to see him.

My fondest love, sweet one, and kisses,
From your very own
AGNES

My Own Dearest One,

I am so busy that I know not how to turn round. My brother is here helping to pack. Frank wishes to know, dear one, what you would like him to give you. Either a *watch* or a jewel case. He is very anxious to give you something for your own use. I think you will find a watch most useful about the Parish. He is to give me a travelling bag which I shall take to Folkestone.

The sky is as black as my coat so I expect to get a wetting. They are all coming over from Bath tomorrow and from Westbury so we shall be a goodly party. I wish you could be here too, dear. Not much longer now – Hurrah.

> With fondest love,
> He is her own
> ARTHUR

Glen Luie, 11 September 1881

My Darling Arthur,

I have been to school today for the last time, I suppose, as a single girl. It was so hard for me to bear, for my children were sobbing bitterly all the afternoon; it was quite useless trying to give them a lesson. They are all coming to the Temperance Meeting on Tuesday when the old women are going to present me with a gold pencil case. It is good of them. How awfully good of Francis to give me something, it seems too good to be true. I shall of course choose a watch as I haven't one and I'm afraid I should never get sufficient jewels to fill a case. I am going to write to Bath tonight – be sure and tell me if you leave Bristol before Wednesday or I shall not know where to direct your letter. Don't forget, dear one, to bring my bouquet – a very jolly one. I can hardly believe that this is my last Sunday. Papa and Mother feel my leaving home very much, so knowing this, I screw up all my courage and appear so awfully lively before them. I am so happy to think you really love me and you know, dear one, that I really do love you very dearly or I could never marry you and I shall try and do my utmost to make you happy. It is, darling, an awfully solemn thing to bind yourself to one person for life if you don't love each other. But I shall have no feelings of this kind. She does love him so fondly. I went to the early service this morning and had breakfast at the vicarage. The Vicar and Mrs Strange were here yesterday and we had a game of tennis. I shall be awfully busy tomorrow. Don't I long for Wednesday. I shall watch for your cab – come straight up.

Fondest love, sweetheart,
Ever your very own
AGNES

Colston Parade, 11 September 1881

My Own Dearest One,

They are all coming over from Bath to services today being my last Sunday and I do not know when I shall be able to write to you so I am doing so now. I was somehow expecting the Sunday School were going to give me a little present. I don't know why I thought so but they have not done so this morning.

Fancy the 13th Sunday after Trinity has arrived at last. This day week we shall be spending it together – how *delightful*. How sweet her letter was this morning!! I do so *long* to see her and press her to my heart.

Goodbye, dear love,
Your own
ARTHUR

My Very Dearest One,

I am in the midst of confusion. Francis has been helping me all the morning getting my things packed. The men are coming soon to pack my furniture. He thinks she has made a very wise choice about Francis' present. She will find a watch most useful. He is going to give me a travelling bag – shan't I feel swell with it? Francis got a letter this morning to say he was to be sent on detachment so he may have to go any day. About the gloves, they will do exactly as you wish and therefore will wear white. The men are taking off my books and making the room look more miserable than ever. Oh, shan't I be glad when all this is over. Fancy the day after tomorrow I shall see my love again, to be parted never more. Oh, it is too splendid almost to be true. It is lucky there is a good number of us going together on Wednesday or I don't know what would become of me. I should be jumping out of the window or something else as mad. Excuse the blotch – it was all the packer's fault, stupid man. You cannot think how wretched my room looks nor how happy I feel.

> With fondest love to my own true one,
> He is her very own
> ARTHUR

[And so, on the 15th September 1881, Arthur and Agnes were joined in holy matrimony in Holy Trinity Church in Southampton. They went off by train in the late afternoon to spend their honeymoon in Folkestone. From there in October, they travelled to Barley in Cambridgeshire where Arthur took up his curacy, carrying a stipend of £150 a year, and where the small house which they had written about so often in their letters was waiting for them.

They were very hard up, although 'Donnie' always maintained that she saved £100 during their first year of marriage. However, it is clear from the following few letters of Bessie Bowers to her daughter that she happily subsidised the Barley household in cash and kind.]

Bessie Bowers, 'Donnie's' mother

Glen Luie, 24 February 1882

My Dear Don,

I am not going to send your parcel tomorrow, I have had rheuma-
tism in my knee and not able to go down town, but it is better
today so that I shall pack it early next week and also send you a
little Post Office order out of my dividends. I went to see if my
butcher could pack a nice silver-side of corn beef; it comes in so
nicely for breakfast or supper, then you can put a nice thick piece
of brown paper round the ham and hang it up until the beef is
finished. You must be careful with your heel, you should rest
it entirely until it is well.

Now Don you must not worry about a baby coming. We
will not say anything about small clothes for a month or two,
then, if then, your dear Mother will arrange. Fancy Arthur a
father! It will be sure to be pretty having Papa and Mama's
beauty combined . . . Now, pets, God bless you both and with
fondest love from all.

Believe me,
Your loving Mother,
BESSIE BOWERS

Glen Luie, 4 March 1882

My Darling Children,

I enclose you a P.O.O. for five pounds, also 31/- for drinking
money, making a total of £6.11.0; it will my pets, help to fill
some little corners.

Now, dears, your hamper will leave here carriage paid on Wednesday morning next. Brown is curing you a piece of beef and will send it on Wednesday morning fit for packing. You will find a packet of large acidulated drops which you will find a great comfort; keep one in your mouth. It did Amy so much good also a little weak soda and brandy. Never mind the expense, your Mother will send you more. Answer this letter by return of post and also tell me how your little stock of wine and spirits stand, I am sure it must be getting low. I do hope you will both be able to come to us after Easter.

My dear Donnie, will you order a small cask of stout, I like Bell* to have it for supper. Dr Hope says she must take it and I am sure it will do Arthur good. I expect I shall have to send Bell a little money before she returns, then she shall pay for the stout. Now, my pets, God bless you and with fondest love from all.

Believe me,
Your loving Mother,
BESSIE BOWERS

[But the expected years of wedded bliss in Barley for which Agnes and Arthur had planned and prepared were soon to be cut short. Less than a year later, Arthur was appointed to a new curacy in the parish of Gainsborough in Lincolnshire. And by then they knew that Donnie was expecting a baby.]

---

* Mrs Bowers's name for Bella, Agnes's sister.

My Darling Children,

Papa is going to Barrow in Furness early on Monday morning and I do not know exactly when he will return and as Amy left you so shortly and you will soon be here, I am going to Bristol on Monday and I think I shall remain until you both arrive at Mrs Thorndike's, but if I do not I shall go and see them. My dear Don, I am so pleased you are going to Gainsborough. We think Arthur is perfectly right, he is far too good for Barley. Tell him not to care a dump for any of the Barley time. I think Papa is writing to Arthur today, he has been so busy. If you suffer with a pain in your back take a warm bath; you should have a bath every morning, it would do you so much good. It was nothing but my baths that did me good when I was in your position, and great walks. You have nothing to get nervous about and nothing to trouble about. Now, darlings, good night, we no doubt shall meet at Bristol or Bath, so with fondest love in which they all join,

Believe me,
Your loving Mother,
BESSIE BOWERS

My Precious Children,

Dear Amy will be with you on Tuesday, then my mind will be easy. Dottie comes to me on Monday; she will be well cared for and James will be here every day. Now, my darlings, do not provide anything for Wednesday or Thursday, there will be enough in Grannie's basket. I shall also send you 2 bottles of Brandy, 2 Whiskey, 2 Gin, 2 Port, 2 Sherry and 2 of Champagne for Bell's wedding day or you may require a little while you are poorly. I am going to pay Amy's travelling expenses, and any little dainty thing you fancy while she is with you, I have asked her to get. And now, my Donnie, cheer up and think how glad your Mother's heart would be to know it is all over.

Dear Papa is in Scotland. I could not go with him, Robert being expected, the ship has not yet arrived, I suppose it will be home tonight.

Willie is gone to Oxford this morning to attend the law lectures but will come down for Bell's wedding. The Butchers sent her an ivory carving knife and fork and steel set in solid silver and the Campbells a box with 6 dessert knives and forks, so she seems to be getting on nicely. Now, my pets, I am going to write a line to Teddy, then out for a walk, for I feel so dull without my John, so God bless you both and the little one in obscurity, and believe me

Your loving Mother,
BESSIE BOWERS

[Ten days later, on October 24th 1882, Arthur and Agnes' first child was born. She was christened Agnes Sybil.]

Glen Luie, 4 November 1882

My Darling Children,

Another week passed, we have ordered the cloak from Hinds, it will be made by next Thursday, then we are going down to see it before it is sent away. It will be an expensive one, so Donnie you must be careful with it; when it arrives just drop me a line. Now, my Donnie, send me word before Nurse goes and I will send you a little *douer* to assist in paying her. You will miss dear Amy but you will not be dull with sweet Arthur and baby. Is it true her name is to be Isabella Marian? . . . Now, pets, God bless you and with fondest love from all and kisses for Baby,

Believe me,
Your loving Mother,
BESSIE BOWERS

Donnie Thorndike and Sybil, 1882

[After Sybil was born, Arthur seems to have been sent away on and off doing locums for other parishes and visiting his mother in Bath, while Donnie occupied herself happily with the new baby and with social life in Gainsborough.]

The Paragon, 4 December 1882

My Darling One,

I arrived at 6 o'clock in perfect safety, the train did not lose any time on the way, but still it was a long journey. The company I had in my carriage was not of the most refined character. I think one was a monthly nurse, fat with an inflamed boil on one side of her nose. She was eating when I got into the train; her food

141

wrapped up in dirty untidy paper, which she shovelled into her basket in dire confusion. At last she fell asleep and snored loudly; she was awakened from her sleep by the train stopping at Saltey and asked in a sleepy tone of a young man who had just got in whether they made salt here, at which I nearly burst out laughing.

Frank is looking very thin and weak, so very different to what he used to look. Mother is looking well, though anxious about Frank. I have not yet seen Isabella as she is at the bazaar and returns at 10. I wonder, dear old thing, how you are getting on. I hope she has not been grieving. How did she enjoy her dinner. I had a very hurried lunch at Derby where we stopped 10 minutes. It is rather hard to write under the circumstances.

Mother and Frank send fondest love, and with his very best kiss for the dear baby, which he trusts is all right in the bowels,

Your ever loving and affectionate husband,
ARTHUR

Ye Olde Vicarage
Gainsboro'
5 December 1882

My Very Darling Arthur,

Just a few lines duckey to tell you how we are getting on. I have received your letter and feel quite cheered. Baby has been very fretful this morning but seems a little quieter now; her bowels are not right yet, they were greenish this morning: I don't much think of going to the Church. Don't worry about us because if she were worse I should let you know. I have been with the little pet all day. I am so sorry about poor Frank and hope with careful nursing he will soon be himself again. . . . I am anxiously looking forward to Thursday. The gas is flickering to such an extent I can hardly see to write and none of us know how to stop it but we can manage with night lights till you come. Fancy, the day after tomorrow I shall have you with me, how lovely it will be darling, won't it? Your little daughter sends her fondest love and especially to her Uncle Frank. The little pet looked rather pale this morning but I don't think she is any worse. I had her on my arm most of the night. Denford is so kind to us and is with Baby now. Now, darling one, goodbye for the present; please, I want a farthing stick of liquorice and a farthing change.

I am ever your own,
True Wife
DONNIE

The Paragon, 6 December 1882

My Own Wifie,

Tomorrow by this time I hope to be with you. I have just been trying to sing without an accompaniment "The little hero" which was very trying. I wanted my Donnie so much. I was so glad to receive your dear letter this morning. What misery you must be suffering from the gas; why did you not send for Tall to rectify it? Frank has not been nearly so well today; I think he did too much yesterday. I went to fetch the doctor this evening but he was not in so he is coming tomorrow. I have been to the bazaar and 'have bought my sweetheart lots of things, she'll buy them with a kiss I know, for *well* my love loves me'. Sister Julia has been trying to play 'The Lord is mindful of his own' but I could not get on with it so left it and went on with my letter. I hope the dear Baby is no worse. In haste to catch the post.

With best love,
Your loving Husband,
ARTHUR

[Donnie's mother, Bessie Bowers, died in April 1883. Donnie went down to Southampton for the funeral, leaving Arthur in charge at Gainsborough.]

My Dearest One,

The Vicar wrote me a very nice letter this morning in which he expressed his grief at the news of my letter. He said he had thought much of you and had not forgotten you in his prayers. What a charm sympathy has for us especially when in deep trouble. He said the girls had written to you so I expect they told you how very dull they were in Cheltenham. When I arrived last night Elizabeth met me at the door saying that baby was perfectly well and in a few minutes after Denford brought her down looking so bright and happy and smiling; it was quite cheering to see her. Drew came in and had some dinner and then we walked up to the Vicarage. Mrs W was very grieved to hear of dear Grannie's death and also of Amy's weakness and asked us to supper tonight, which will be like paying penance for I shall be in no humour to talk and Drew has not the ability so Mrs W will have to do it all herself. Dear Donnie, I hope you are bearing up bravely against your heavy sorrow and helping dear Amy and Bella to do the same. What pleasure we shall have now in looking forward to Paradise, knowing that we have those there we love so dearly. Do not grieve then, dear, but look forward with joyful hope to meet your dear mother again. Glen Luie has not been out of my mind since I left you. I thought so much of you all at the Holy Communion this morning. I am now off to the Union, so with fondest love to all and plenty of kisses from sleeping Sybil,

Your fond husband,
ARTHUR

[It seems that, in February 1884, Arthur and Donnie left 'Ye Olde Vicarage' and moved to another house in Gainsborough. Arthur, having been prevailed upon to apply for the post of Minor Canon in Rochester, had travelled south for an interview, leaving Donnie to make the move.]

My Sweetest Old Husband,

I arrived quite safely at Mrs Marshall's and she was so delighted
to see us. I came in the bus with baby while Annie and Ada
stopped to lock up the house. Sybil likes her new quarters very
much; our bedroom is the new spare room and furnished very
luxuriously; such a jolly little room leading out of it for Annie.
Sybil woke in the night and had a good cry and Annie came and
walked her about for a few minutes; she soon went off again and
slept until 5 o'clock so I had a better night than usual. Now I must
tell you about the concert. I went at 6 o'clock to practice with
Mr Robinson and the duet went off almost perfectly, everyone
seemed to like it and 'Laddie' was a great success. I was encored
as usual and sang the last verse. The programme was very long;
the dramatic sketch was so long that it was 10 o'clock before it
was over and then we had only commenced the second part so I
asked the Vicar to get me off my second song and with a great
amount of persuasion they did so, for I was so sleepy and felt
quite thankful when the time came to go home. I missed you so
dreadfully in the night especially when the daughter commenced
the first cry, and directly the pet woke she kissed me, then said
'Dada' and looked for you and seemed dreadfully crushed because you were not there. However, I tried to comfort her and
told her that you would soon be home again, that though you
were away, you were telling everybody what a dear little girl
you had and how you loved her. I have been thinking of you so
much this morning and wondering how those old guns are
treating you. I do hope for the best but never mind darling, if
you don't get it, we shall still love each other all the same so
don't think I shall grieve, will you? I am going to take this to the
post myself in case of an accident. I am anxiously looking out for
your letter. Give my fondest love to my little 'sanctum', I can't

ask you to embrace it for, of course, it might give you a stiff neck, so with heaps of love and kisses,

> Ever your loving and devoted,
> WIFIE

P.S. Give our love to Grannie, Isabella and Francis.

> *Cleveland House, 13 February 1884*

My Own Darling Hubby,

You cannot tell how delighted I was to receive the telegram. I knew before I opened it what the news would be and I felt hot and cold at intervals. I sent up the telegram to the Vicarage last night and Mr Williams wrote me such a nice letter, of course saying how sorry he was to lose us but so glad for your sake. The Vicar is coming in presently to have a little talk. You can imagine how anxious I was to get your letter. You did do well, you old pet; did you see the house and what is the place like, I am so anxious to hear; I hope the house is not too large. I am so happy here and Sybil is flourishing. The Vicar took me over the Yoffee Tavern yesterday, it is fitted most splendidly and I was so pleased with it, the rooms are so well furnished. I am just going out for a good walk. Do, pet, tell me about the house and place. Best love to all and heaps of kisses,

> Your loving and fond
> WIFIE

> *Cleveland House, 14 February 1884*

My Darling Hubby,

Just a few lines to tell you we are getting on alright. Last night Mr and Mrs Wright came in to dinner. Mrs W never said a word about you, not even congratulated me on your success, but

146

everybody else did. I had a letter from Amy wanting to know all particulars but of course I cannot tell her as I don't know myself. I am anxious to know what sort of crib we shall have, do tell me. I saw the dear Vicar yesterday, he seems very cut up about our going and hoped they wouldn't want you directly. He wrote me such a nice letter. I am going to the Vicarage this morning with Sybil. Dalton is in a fearful rage about you going, he growled at the Vicar furiously as though it were his fault! I so long for you to come home and tell me everything. I hope you arrived at Bath safely, I am expecting a letter today. Goodbye, my pet, until we meet. Fondest love and kisses from your loving little,

WIFIE

The Paragon, 15 February 1884

My Own Darling Wifie,

I am going down to Rochester again to see a little about the house. I leave here tonight and stay with the Thorndikes, leave at 8.20 and arrive at Rochester at 10.14. Start from Liverpool Street at 4.22 and arrive home at 8.22. I had such a rush after I knew I was appointed Minor Canon to catch the 3.57 that I never thought of remaining another night, especially as I was anxious to get down to Bath to see Frank before he went*; so I think it best to go down again before I return home to make necessary arrangements; it will save me coming down again. I hope the inside of the house is more promising than the outside. We have been hard at work this morning getting Frank's things packed, he leaves at 6.33 tonight. Only another day and I shall be able to tell you all about the place. I have not had time to write to the Vicar. The Dean will leave it entirely to the Vicar about my time of leaving but they would like me to come as soon as I could. I said I could not well come till after Easter as there would be so much work to be done during Lent and at Easter.

---

* Frank was setting off with his regiment for India, where, alas, he died not very long after of cholera.

All send best love to their Donnie and Sybil, and with much from her ever

Devoted Husband,
ARTHUR

Royal Mail Steam Packet Company
Engineers Department
Southampton
22 February 1884

My Dear Arthur and Donnie,

I have just time to write a few lines in reply to your letters of the 18th and 20th inst.

After the 25th of March I will be able to let you have what money you require to avoid trouble and bank charges. I will write you a long letter if possible tomorrow. In the meantime I am very pleased with the prospects before you and congratulate you upon your success at Rochester.

I hope this will find you all in good health. How is my dear little grand daughter.

With much love to you all and kisses for Sybil,
I am,
My Dear Arthur and Donnie,
Your loving Father
J. BOWERS

12 Boley Hill
Rochester
24 April 1884

My Own Darling Wifie,

I received your two letters today making up for not having one yesterday. I am very sorry to hear dear Amy is so bad. I hope it is not really bronchitis. When is Eliza coming to me? I cannot get the house quite straight without a servant. What a delight it will be to have you with me again to arrange the house, etc. The pantechnicon company object to reduce the charge and I fear there is no help for it, we must pay it. I reserved £35 out of the £100. I shall pay him this and he must wait for the rest. Give my love to Amy and don't let her worry. Take things easy, they will come right and don't you, old lady, be nervous; I can see by your letter you are quite worrying. I hope your Father's head is not very bad. With a kiss for the darling child and for my own sweet wife,

Your ever devoted,
Husband ARTHUR

[At last Donnie left Gainsborough and, with the baby Sybil, set off for Bath to visit Arthur's mother before finally going to her new home in Rochester.]

The Paragon, 25 April 1884

My Own Darling Arthur,

I arrived here safely at 4 o'clock. Grannie met us at the station and was so charmed with Sybil, she is a darling pet and she can say heaps of words. Dottie has brought her out considerably. I suppose, darling, you have sent my letter to Southampton so that I shall not receive it until tomorrow. Grannie says I must stay for the Fancy Fair on Wednesday, it is to be a very grand affair. I shall leave it entirely to you, dear, to decide; if you feel very lonely and want me very much I will come to you on Monday but Grannie has set her heart on my staying so, dear, you write and tell me what I am to do. I left dear Amy very poorly but Dr Lake assured me that there was nothing serious, only a very severe chill, but I feel very unhappy at leaving her; but I felt bound to come. I will get Eliza Ann to meet me in London if you cannot. I shall come home next Thursday if you do not want me before. Goodnight, my darling. Fondest love and kisses from your,

Very fond WIFIE and SYBIL

P.S. Take great care of the cold. I asked Dr Lake about your throat and he says by no means have it cut! I shall kiss it shorter!

Boley Hill, 26 April 1884

My Own Darling Donnie,

I am so glad to hear you have arrived safely in Bath, it does look now more like coming home. Of course, dear, you must stay for the Fancy Fair, only don't let any one take you for a fancy piece of goods and run off with you. Tomorrow I make my debut in the Cathedral by taking the litany in the morning service and helping in the celebration at mid-day. In the afternoon I take the service in the nave. Canon Money preaches, as it is Hospital Sunday, and the Mayor and Corporation all come in their scarlet so it will be a pretty sight, reminding one of Redcliffe on Whitsundays.

Tonight is the grand rehearsal, 1/- admission; they expect to turn away a couple of hundred who will not be able to squeeze in. I must now close, with best love to dear Mother and Isabella and with kisses for the darling pet and a hug for the dearest little wife.

Ever your devoted,
Husband ARTHUR

My Precious Arthur,

I was so delighted with your letter this morning, I wrote you yesterday but as no letters are delivered in London on Sunday I fear you will not get it until Monday. It will not be much longer now for you to be without me, be sure you let me know about your coming to meet me, if not I must get somebody, as you know what a courageous wifie you possess. Poor dear Grannie looks sadly altered, she has suffered so with her teeth and hasn't the slightest appetite. I saw such a change in her, she looks quite breaking up. Grannie is delighted with baby. She certainly is a pet, though at the present moment she has woke up from her sleep very cross. If you would care to run down to Bath on Wednesday and go back with us I would pay your expenses, as Papa gave me a little tip. I will tell you all about the theatre when I come home. I will write you tomorrow, darling. Think of me Artie and I shall be thinking of you tomorrow night singing; don't hurt your throat.

Heaps of kisses, dear one,
Your own fond
WIFIE

My Own Darling Arthur,

I am going to lunch with Sister Julia so write you a few lines before I go. Be sure you let me know about Thursday, I have written to Eliza; if she doesn't arrive before I come, you must get a woman in; have a fire, dear, in the kitchen, also dining room if it is cold and don't forget, dear, to get in something to eat; also some milk for Sybil. We are longing to see you again. Grannie is a little better but still very poorly, she has such wretched sickness – of course it cannot be the 'family way'. We are going to the theatre tonight to see a romantic Irish drama. I couldn't let you be gay, you see dear, without plunging into gaiety myself. My thoughts will be with you, dear, how I long to see you my duckey; I have made so many resolutions when I get home, I hope I shan't break them. Goodbye for the present, darling. We send heaps of love and kisses, darling, and I am always your devoted

WIFIE

The Paragon, 29 April 1884

My Own Darling Husband,

If it is inconvenient to you dear, do not come to London and meet me, I have written to Eliza Ann to meet me at Paddington. Don't you think if there were a train leaving Victoria about 5 o'clock it would do nicely? I am longing, my darling, to see you, it seems years to me since we met; how thankful I shall be, dear one, to get to my own home. I am very happy here but there is such a dreadful want which only my Artie can supply. I never spent such a long fortnight in my life. We went to the theatre last night – it was rather good. Sybil can say several more words and keeps saying 'No, no' and shaking her head, you will be pleased with her. Now, darling, I shall write to you tomorrow and let you know about Thursday. Fondest love and kisses, darling one, from

your fond WIFIE and SYBIL

[The move to Rochester was a major undertaking, but Donnie appears to have managed very philosophically over the constant moves that took place during their early years. It was obviously a tremendous joy and relief to them both when they found themselves established in Rochester in May 1884 with Arthur now a Minor Canon of the Cathedral.]

The photograph on the preceding page,
taken in April 1897, shows
Canon and Mrs Arthur Thorndike
with Sybil, Eileen and Frank

POSTSCRIPT

by John Casson

In Rochester Arthur and Donnie were blessed with three more children: Russell in 1884, Eileen in 1890 and Frank in 1894, and they all lived happily together in Minor Canon Row in the Cathedral precincts. From all accounts they were a lively family. The children played charades and acted plays in the attic. Arthur led them in singsongs with his rich baritone voice, while Agnes played the piano to them and for them with boisterous vigour, accompanied by her own penetrating soprano.

Soon after Eileen's birth Arthur was made vicar of St Margaret's, the largest parish in Rochester. The expanded living space in the huge vicarage expanded their hearts and minds. They were a very close family who preferred each other's company to that of anybody else, and to themselves they were very special people.

In 1900 Arthur took over the parish of Aylesford, seven miles away from Rochester and in the lovely country along the Medway. From here the children went their several ways. Sybil and Russell went off to be actors while Eileen and Frank, still young children prepared themselves to do the same. And on the 22nd December 1908 Sybil was married in Aylesford Church to Lewis Casson. It was almost the last family occasion in Aylesford, for a few months later Arthur, having been made an honorary canon of Rochester, became Vicar of St James the Less in Pimlico. He and Donnie moved into a spacious vicarage at No. 75 St George's Square, where in October 1909 I, John Casson, Sybil's first child and their first grandchild, was born.

By 1916, Sybil and Lewis had four children and for a time, because of the war, we all lived in the vicarage. They say I once told a visitor that we liked being with Granny because 'she makes everybody feel jolly.'

On Sunday evening December 9th 1917, Donnie had gone off early to the church to prepare her organ playing at evensong. Arthur lingered a little at the vicarage to finish his sermon.

He left it rather late and had to run some of the way to church. As the choir moved into the church Arthur, walking behind them, fell back into the vestry and died of a heart attack a few minutes later. Donnie, hastily summoned from her organ, arrived just too late and knelt beside him crying, 'I've loved you for 36 years, darling, don't leave me.'

She was well-nigh inconsolable and never really recovered from Arthur's death. But her indomitable spirits and energy kept her going for another 15 years. We remember her throughout our childhood as a marvellous if eccentric grandmother

Donnie Thorndike in about 1925

whom we all adored. She became a familiar sight in Chelsea where we all lived, her ample figure draped in flowing light grey silk with a huge hat to match, and a silver cross, given her by Arthur, on a chain round her neck which clanked loudly on her string of beads.

Now, one hundred years after their wedding, Arthur and Donnie lie together in the churchyard of their adored Aylesford. And the ashes of their first child, Sybil, lie under the South Aisle of Westminster Abbey.